# Seeing Good, Doing Evil

# Seeing Good, Doing Evil

The Limits of Moral Ignorance

MICHAEL D. RUSSELL

*foreword by Andrew Cameron*

WIPF & STOCK · Eugene, Oregon

SEEING GOOD, DOING EVIL
The Limits of Moral Ignorance

Copyright © 2020 Michael D. Russell. All rights reserved. Except for brief quotations in critical publications or reviews, no part of this book may be reproduced in any manner without prior written permission from the publisher. Write: Permissions, Wipf and Stock Publishers, 199 W. 8th Ave., Suite 3, Eugene, OR 97401.

Unless specified otherwise, English Biblical quotations are from THE HOLY BIBLE: NEW INTERNATIONAL VERSION®. NIV®. Copyright © 1973, 1978, 1984, 2011 by International Bible Society, www.ibs.org. All rights reserved worldwide.

Where specified as NRSV, quotations are taken from the New Revised Standard Version Bible: Catholic Edition, copyright © 1989, 1993 National Council of the Churches of Christ in the United States of America. Used by permission. All rights reserved worldwide.

Greek Biblical quotations are from Novum Testamentum Graece, Nestle-Aland 27th Edition. Copyright (c) 1993 Deutsch Bibelgesellschaft, Stuttgart.

Wipf & Stock
An Imprint of Wipf and Stock Publishers
199 W. 8th Ave., Suite 3
Eugene, OR 97401

www.wipfandstock.com

PAPERBACK ISBN: 978-1-7252-7591-1
HARDCOVER ISBN: 978-1-7252-7592-8
EBOOK ISBN: 978-1-7252-7593-5

Manufactured in the U.S.A.   07/28/20

To Alison

# Contents

*Foreword by Andrew Cameron* — ix

*Acknowledgments* — xv

*Abbreviations* — xvii

Chapter 1  Introduction: The Limits of Moral Ignorance — 1

Chapter 2  Unifying the Concepts of General Revelation and Natural Law — 7

Chapter 3  Testing Propositions against the Text of Romans 1 and 2 — 20

Chapter 4  A Theological Anthropology Focused on Perception — 47

Chapter 5  Philosophical-Ethical Perspectives — 63

Chapter 6  Applications for Confident Presentation of the Gospel — 81

Chapter 7  Conclusion — 98

*Bibliography* — 109

# Foreword

> Thus says the LORD:
> "For three transgressions of the Ammonites,
>   and for four, I will not revoke the punishment;
>   because they have ripped open pregnant women in Gilead
>   in order to enlarge their territory.
> So I will kindle a fire against the wall of Rabbah,
>   fire that shall devour its strongholds,
> with shouting on the day of battle,
>   with a storm on the day of the whirlwind."[1]

Modern ideologues who oppose all retributive justice will object to the divine judgment in this passage. But even given the modern queasiness around divine judgment, the rest of us may have some sympathy with Amos. To destroy social institutions that set the conditions for genocide by feticide, all conducted simply to expand territory, resonates with our modern loathing of "crimes against humanity." If we approved air strikes against the Serbian killers in Kosovo, we shouldn't be too troubled by Amos.

Amos makes no suggestion that these poor Ammonites lacked the law of God, and so were confused about genocide. Ancient and modern readers alike can intuit evil here. Something about the landscape of human existence "presses in," bringing to us forms of moral knowledge that need no statute.

Except, it seems, for the Ammonite soldiers on the day. As they methodically hunted down each desperate pregnant woman, enough did not press upon them to prevent them. It is a common enough story in war: My Lai, Malmedy, the Katyn Forest, and Gilead. No one really does anything without a reason; all behavior has meaning; and like every violent man

---

1. Amos 1:13–14, NRSV.

before and after them, these Ammonites knew how so to dehumanize their quarry as to elevate some preferred ideal—in this case, the tempting lands of Gilead. Like all violent men before and after them, they knew how to love their unit, their cadre, their tribe, in ways that "justified" this action. Their truth was right for them.

Of course to us, it is too much of a stretch to question whether they were morally culpable. These were, after all, pregnant women. In those inchoate scales of value that we all carry (rightly or wrongly), no human being can be more precious than the pregnant woman. Those soldiers deserved all their nation got, or so we should think if we also spare no quarter to "good" Nazi camp guards and their nation at the time. Despite that we may envisage how he and they could have been trapped into cycles of violence, nationwide groupthink, honor codes of obedience, and Hitlerian deception, we judge them all corrupt.

Yet what of those infractions a little less severe, and closer to home? As I write, a well-regarded Australian bank executive has stepped down after his organization committed twenty-three million reporting infractions concerning financial transactions that included payments to child sex-traffickers. But he did not know; his organization's culture was not up to keeping up; how culpable is he?

Still closer to home, our personal infractions almost always seem right. Psychologists speak of "attribution bias," where we are very hard on the motives of others, and very easy on our own. The sixteenth-century theologian John Calvin knew well this natural-born human "skill" of excuse-making:

> The intellect is very rarely deceived in general [but] is illusory when it goes farther, that is, applies the principle to particular cases. In reply to the general question, every man will affirm that murder is evil. But he who is plotting the death of an enemy contemplates murder as something good. The adulterer will condemn adultery in general, but will privately flatter himself in his own particular adultery.[2]

The matter of culpability becomes even more fraught when it comes to belief, or not, in God. After all, with all the options out there, who is to say? For those whom we might call "naturalists," scientific stories have generated stories more plausible than God concerning how our existence came to be. Equally, the biblical proposal that the love of a good God pervades all[3] seems so unlikely to some during times of suffering, that God has come to seem so remote and unloving as to collapse into nonexistence.

2. Calvin, *Institutes*, II.ii.23.
3. Psalm 33:5.

Most of us are sympathetic, then, to the view that perhaps people in these straits cannot seriously be expected to sense God, let alone honor God. Yet especially for Christians of "Reformed Protestant" persuasion, St. Paul's famous declaration in Romans 1:18–21 looms very large. According to this first-century manifesto, what can be known about God—and by extension, about ethics—is plain to people, so we are "without excuse" in the face of that same menace of divine wrath as confronted the Ammonites. They should have known enough about pregnant-woman-ripping to know not to do it. So also we, Paul proposes, are without excuse when God confronts us for whatever beliefs and actions seemed good to us on the day, but weren't.

In our time, this notion has come to seem at least unpalatable, and more likely unbelievable. Michael Russell's book is an extended meditation on the possibilities in this Pauline statement and a concerted effort to enable us to understand and accept it. Situated in Reformed Protestant discussion of this matter, he offers some clarifying proposals. Maintaining all the while that whoever we are, we are indeed without excuse, Michael proposes how to understand that conclusion without accepting some of the usual routes to it. His suggestions are surprising.

Concerning what we may reasonably be expected to know, he suggests that theological tradition has made too large a distinction between "natural theology" and "natural law." This distinction always seemed reasonable to theological thinkers because it is harder to intuit things about the uncreated and transcendent One than to intuit the preciousness of pregnant women. For some thinkers therefore, ignorance of the divine might inherently be more defensible than "ignorance" about, say, the evils of genocide. Michael rejects such claims by contending that connection to God is actually a species of what was sometimes called "practical reason," the kind of reasoning that has more to do with doing than with mere thinking.

It seems to him that the created order delivers an entire package of what he will term "legal revelation"—a composite map of divine and moral reality that over time, "presses in on us," making it both thinkable and liveable to respond to God, and to question and challenge our own particular casual evils. Although the term "legal revelation" initially sounds odd, it is inspired by a reading of Luther and makes increasing sense as Michael unfolds his argument.

Significantly, his account denies some inborn "sense of the divine" (*sensus divinatus*), as Calvinists term it. He suggests that we must take more seriously the atheist's self-revelation when she insists that she really and truly neither sees nor feels any reason to believe in God. If we assume that in the first instance she is not lying to herself about her lack of a sense of the divine, then the harder task becomes determining how Paul remains correct to say that she is "without excuse." Respecting this atheist's self-report, Michael sets about that harder task. The main body of the book necessarily includes some close and technical argument outlining the nuances of a new account of how culpability works.

But if Michael is right, some very prosaic outcomes follow. For example we need commit no "power move" in apologetics, whereby we assert that deep down, others really do know God, despite whatever they say about themselves. Michael suggests there are better ways to discuss the matter with her. His sixth and seventh chapters will assist Christians to engage with neighbors in new and interesting ways.

Michael's book so focuses on the nature of culpability and the certainty of divine judgment that modern readers may be repelled. That repulsion is no fault of Michael's, and has everything to do with our own desires, dispositions, and self-narratives. But to focus closely on his account and to find ourselves truly "without excuse" is finally to know ourselves as morally serious beings. We carry within us the complement of God's profound and unrelenting expectation for authentic response to God and to what surrounds us. To be "without excuse" is to matter, and to know that we matter.

Even so, lest this focus suggest that theology only deals in culpability and judgment, we will approach Michael's book via the thirteenth chapter of the intertestamental Book of Wisdom. Although not considered canonical Scripture by Protestant Christians, Wisdom has traditionally been regarded as a good read anyway. It anticipates the themes St. Paul expands upon in his opening to the letter to the Romans. For the author of Wisdom:

> [A]ll people who were ignorant of God were foolish by nature; and they were unable from the good things that are seen to know the one who exists, nor did they recognize the artisan while paying heed to his works; but they supposed that either fire or wind or swift air, or the circle of the stars, or turbulent water, or the luminaries of heaven were the gods that rule the world.
>
> If through delight in the beauty of these things people assumed them to be gods, let them know how much better than these is their Lord, for the author of beauty created them. And if people were amazed at their power and working, let them perceive from them how much more powerful is the one who formed them. For from the greatness and beauty of created things comes a corresponding perception of their Creator.[4]

---

4. Wis 13:1–5, NRSV.

The author then "backs off" a little, in a manner reminiscent of St. Paul before the Areopagus:[5]

> Yet these people are little to be blamed, for perhaps they go astray while seeking God and desiring to find him. For while they live among his works, they keep searching, and they trust in what they see, because the things that are seen are beautiful.[6]

Those sentiments are a little too "optimistic" for many Reformed Protestants, and probably even for the St. Paul of "without excuse." However the author then reverses himself:

> Yet again, not even they are to be excused; for if they had the power to know so much that they could investigate the world, how did they fail to find sooner the Lord of these things?[7]

Like St. Paul, this author goes on to condemn the stupidity of handmade idols as a way to express our hunches about God. But he knows that human stupidity, frailty of vision, and unacknowledged culpability before a just God is, emphatically, not the final word:

> But you are merciful to all, for you can do all things, and you overlook people's sins, so that they may repent. For you love all things that exist, and detest none of the things that you have made, for you would not have made anything if you had hated it. How would anything have endured if you had not willed it? Or how would anything not called forth by you have been preserved? You spare all things, for they are yours, O Lord, you who love the living. [. . .] Although you are sovereign in strength, you judge with mildness, and with great forbearance you govern us.[8]

This merciful One St. Paul came to know more fully in the person, work, and face of Jesus Christ. This is also the God whom Michael wishes us all to know—someone from whom we have no need to flee into lame excuses and who longs for us to ditch our failed excuses and find instead connection, beauty, mercy, and joy.

Andrew Cameron
St. Mark's National Theological Centre
Barton, ACT, Australia
6th December 2019

---

5. Acts 17.
6. Wis 13:6–7, NRSV.
7. Wis 13:9, NRSV.
8. Wis 11:23–26; 12:18, NRSV.

# Acknowledgments

I would like to acknowledge the vast amount of help I have received from various quarters in the production of this work. First, the supervisors of my thesis, from which this book derives: Brian Edgar, Kevin Kinghorn, Chad Thornhill, and Jeff Pugh, have all contributed in various important ways. Thanks also go to my thesis markers, Andrew Cameron and Scott Harrower. Andrew was very kind to write so many incisive and pertinent suggestions that helped the final publication substantially. He was kinder still to write the foreword to this publication. Various turns of phrase, suggestions, and influences from all of these men appear throughout, yet the argument and ideas remain my own. When the thesis was floundering somewhat, it was Jeff's brilliant advice, both in the detail, and especially in the overall shaping of the thesis, that enabled the work to come together with far greater cohesion than I could achieve alone.

I am very thankful too for my church, St. George's Magill, affording me the time to write. My wife, Alison, has been a glorious support as I have laboured in writing, and is such a delight to me. Thanks also go to Anthony Roe, Jennifer Russell and Bronwyn Lund for their proofreading work, Emily Callihan for her copyediting, and Wipf and Stock Publishers as a whole. Their team was gracious enough to accept this manuscript for publication, and they worked in a friendly and professional fashion in achieving this outcome. Above all, I'm thankful to the Lord Jesus, whose sacrifice stands as my major motivation in writing, as well as the content to which I trust this work points.

Michael D. Russell

# Abbreviations

## BIBLICAL BOOKS

| | |
|---|---|
| Gen | Genesis |
| Exod | Exodus |
| Lev | Leviticus |
| Deut | Deuteronomy |
| Ps | Psalms |
| Isa | Isaiah |
| Dan | Daniel |
| Matt | Matthew |
| Rom | Romans |
| Phil | Philippians |
| Col | Colossians |
| 1–2 Cor | 1–2 Corinthians |
| 1–2 Pet | 1–2 Peter |

## OTHER ABBREVIATIONS

| | |
|---|---|
| NRSV | New Revised Standard Version |
| Wis | Book of Wisdom |

# Chapter 1

# Introduction

## *The Limits of Moral Ignorance*

### STATING THE QUESTION

There is a short stretch of road near where I used to live that is popular for parking. I have been fined twice for parking there without a permit. I remember staring at the confusing set of signs on the second occasion, before concluding, falsely, that I was allowed to park there at that time. Yet more recently still, my wife, Alison, parked successfully a few meters away. She saw clearly where she could and couldn't legally park, in a way I couldn't on two occasions. I still wonder at the clarity of the signage, and therefore at the justice of my two fines. Alison has no issue with the signage.

This work is a study of the limits of our moral ignorance. It is a study of how our limited ability to see what is evil bears on our culpability when we fail to do what is good. The major question then is this: if neither general revelation nor natural law are accessible to people reliably, how can God justly judge them for their ignorance and hold them morally culpable for failing to live according to revelation they cannot reliably access?

By "general revelation" I mean "truths about God that can be known through nature."[1] By "natural law" I mean "truths about ethical universals

---

1. General revelation is best considered a post-Reformation term. B. A. Gerrish

that can be known through nature."[2] So I am asking, if neither God's universal self-revelation, nor truths about ethical universals, are reliably accessible through nature, how can God justly judge people for failing to worship him and keep his law, when they are ignorant?

The sharpness of the question can be seen in a famous exchange involving Bertrand Russell. Russell was asked what he would say if God appeared to him after his death and demanded to know why he had failed to believe. His response was, "Not enough evidence, God. Not enough evidence."[3] Russell's implication is that God cannot justly judge people for their ignorance of him, because God's self-revelation is not clear enough. In parallel fashion, there are many today who might claim that there is insufficient evidence that people should be humble, or chaste, or sober, or hard-working, or possess other character traits, or obey certain moral commands. Those who get these matters wrong might plan to say to God on the Last Day, "Not enough evidence, God! Not enough evidence!" Our assumption is that "people are without excuse,"[4] so that such excuses are not viable. But why are they not viable? How should one respond to a challenge like that of Bertrand Russell?

To tackle the question, one needs to deal with a wide array of issues, for there are a great many relevant pieces to the puzzle. Plainly neither God's general revelation nor his natural law are perceived perfectly by all, for we have so much disagreement on these matters, and there is even disagreement about such matters within the ranks of believers. If this is not because God has been insufficiently clear, why is it? In analyzing culpability for our failures to respond to general revelation and natural law, two broad considerations are important: first, from God's side, the character of his communication, and second, from our side, the way we receive it.

---

describes the development of the notion of general revelation this way: "It is Luther's version of the two-fold knowledge of God that is formalized in seventeenth-century Protestant scholasticism as the contrast between general revelation and special revelation." Gerrish, "Errors and Insights," 66.

2. Rupert Kilcullen, for example, describes the notion of natural law as "the universal and immutable law to which the laws of human legislators, the customs of particular communities and the actions of individuals ought to conform." Our more abbreviated form captures sufficient of this essence for our introductory purpose. Kilcullen, "Natural Law," 831.

3. Salmon, "Religion and Science," 176.

4. Romans 1:20.

## SOME RELEVANT CONSIDERATIONS

One can choose from a wide range of relevant issues in trying to untangle the problem. By way of a representative sample, I have chosen seven, which are by no means exhaustive. First, the scope and content of natural law impacts human culpability, for one needs to be clear on what is required of humans, ethically, to rightly understand our culpability. One question regarding natural law is whether *commands* exhaust its content, or whether broader conceptions are necessary. I will contend that natural law's scope cannot be captured purely in terms of commands, seen for example in that generosity rests on a scale from "more generous" to "less generous," where a particular "less generous" act is not for that reason necessarily a disobedient act.

Second, our level of control in the relevant circumstances impacts human culpability. For example, where God's ethical requirements address our beliefs, our emotions, our contentment, our joy, or other matters which seem beyond our immediate control, the question can be raised as to just how we can be held culpable when we transgress. It is not obvious that culpability can rest on people for their failures in areas which they do not immediately control.

Third, the overlap between natural law and general revelation impacts how one should answer the question. The two notions, which are broadly ethical and theological, respectively, have historically been treated separately, but I will consider whether this has been unfortunate. I will argue that in fact these two notions are best treated as a single notion, since right understanding of the theological demands an ethical response, and since ethical requirements rest on underlying realities, including theological ones. I will call this single notion "legal revelation."

Fourth, the question of the difficulty of perceiving God's general revelation and natural law is relevant to human culpability. There is a host of literature presenting complicated arguments, using specialized evidence, for particular claims of general revelation or natural law. For example, in defending the truth of one premise of his cosmological argument for God's existence, William Lane Craig discusses whether quantum physics furnishes an exception to the truth of his premise and whether the "so-called B-theory of time" might do the same.[5] In defending the truth of his second premise, Craig argues inductively from Einstein's general theory of relativity and discusses the Big Bang and alternative theories such as the oscillating universe and the chaotic inflationary universe.[6] If such complex argument

---

5. Moreland and Craig, *Philosophical Foundations*, 469.
6. Moreland and Craig, *Philosophical Foundations*, 476–77.

and specialized evidence were required to grasp that God exists, it would seem that the unintelligent, or those without access to specialized evidence, might have an excuse for not believing in God, namely that they could not understand the argument. In that case it would seem that God's condemnation of them for unbelief would be unfair. I will contend that God's "legal revelation" is designed to be received in "short and easy" fashion, so that this excuse is unviable.

Fifth, the corporate nature of our reception of ethical reality is relevant to human culpability, since we develop our ethical understandings, character, and practice in families and societies. When our forebears have contributed to our misconception of God's law, the question can be asked whether we can be held fully culpable. I will argue that culpability for an individual's misconceptions of God's law indeed extends beyond the individual to those who raised us, the society we grow up in, and indeed back to Adam and Eve.

Sixth, the nature of sin's distortion of our perception of ethical reality is relevant to human culpability. If human nature is such that we all *inherit* an ingrained tendency to misconceive ethical reality, it can be asked whether we should be held culpable for that which we received at birth. I will argue that we can be held culpable, but that our culpability is shared with our forebears.

Seventh, our psychological development is relevant to our culpability. For the *dynamic* way in which we come, from birth through to adulthood, to correctly perceive *then* misconceive the same ethical realities, *then* move closer in some ways but further away in others, bears on how our culpability should be assessed. The findings of psychologists in these dynamic questions point to where we might bear culpability for misconceiving general revelation and natural law. I will interact with the field of object relations theory from analytic psychology to address this issue.

## THE QUESTION'S IMPORTANCE

It should be clear that the question has many complications. Yet it is an eminently worthwhile question. An accurate answer will help in many ways, perhaps the foremost regarding the way Christians should speak, publicly and privately, when ethical and theological matters are disputed. The current climate in the cultural West is one where all sorts of disagreement can be expected, on all sorts of ethical matters. This is especially so in matters such as sexuality, the nature of gender and gender roles, matters of the value of human life, identity claims and their ethical importance, the devotion due to God, the character traits we should value, and more. Given the importance of this matter, towards the end of this exploration I will provide an argumentation strategy to help apologists, based on my findings.

## THE APPROACH

I will tackle the question by systematically exploring it through a variety of foci. I have chosen this approach because the complexity of the topic means that a linear progression of argument from chapter to chapter seems impossible. In chapter 2, I will first overview the history of the terms "natural law" and "general revelation." I will then consider Luther's distinction between "legal knowledge" and "evangelical knowledge" and suggest that this distinction, and especially his concept of "legal knowledge," opens the way to unifying the concepts of "natural law" and "general revelation." Using Luther's language the distinction will be proposed between "legal revelation" and "evangelical revelation." I will outline flaws that have arisen in modern apologetic scholarship due to a lack of precision in these areas. I will argue that it makes sense to fuse the doctrines of "natural law" and "general revelation," because God's self-revelation has ethical implications. It also makes sense because natural law and general revelation have a commonality of function, namely that failure to live according to either general revelation or natural law is sufficient to deserve condemnation.

In chapter 3, the focus will turn to the exegesis of parts of Paul's letter to the Romans. The resolution of the present question is not possible without revisiting the historical exegetical approaches to two passages in particular. These passages are, first, the dominant text regarding general revelation, Romans 1:18–32, and, second, the dominant text regarding natural law, Romans 2:14–15. I will first propose five ways to see that the fault lies with humanity rather than God that "legal revelation" is not accessible reliably, and test whether exegesis of key sections of Romans is consistent with these proposals. The proposals will focus on the "short and easy" reception of legal revelation, its universal communication, its flawed internalization in all people, the fault for these flaws resting with *humanity as a whole*, and the manifest nature of God's continued communication.

In chapter 4, the focus will rest on the field of theological anthropology. I will consider the proposal that the notions of "projection" and "introjection" from developmental psychology might be understood as the *internalization* of "legal revelation" that I propose in prior chapters. This venture into the field of psychology, though rarely taken in discussions of general revelation or natural law, is nonetheless a natural and important one. Since I am proposing that certain objective truths press on all people but are unreliably received, it makes sense to see if psychological theory, developed as it is through study of actual people, might posit parallel "unreliable reception" of truth and the reasons which have been presented for this. The point will be to see that a widely-accepted psychological model proposes "short and easy" reception of reality which would be available to all, while also being received inaccurately due to flaws in human character.

In chapter 5, the focus will move to the field of philosophical ethics. I will consider several topics in short turn to give depth to the key notion of "legal revelation." I will discuss the nature of moral obligation, considering whether it is of such a kind that one might expect every human to be subject to common, expressible moral obligations. I will consider which human faculties "legal revelation" might be addressed to, that is, whether God's "legal revelation" targets specific human components, powers, or capacities, such as our mind, our will, or our emotions. The question in view here is whether each human faculty upon which moral requirements are laid needs to be directly addressed by "legal revelation" for us to be rightly held as culpable. I will argue that it does. I will also consider the fixity of "legal revelation," since if it were not fixed, a plausible excuse is that a person cannot be expected to grasp an ethical reality that is ever-changing. I will consider the ease of reception of "legal revelation" with a view to the potential excuse that the content was too difficult for some to grasp. I will argue for a fixity of "legal revelation" with a "short and easy" character to its reception.

In chapter 6, I will outline some of the applications of my proposals. These will include observations about the confidence that it might give apologists and evangelists when they understand that their beliefs are grounded in universal notions of the "good" and the "right" infused in the very being of the world. It will include observations regarding the implications of knowing the relative importance and accessibility of different kinds of truths, gospel truths, truths of "legal revelation," and scientific and other truths. It will include, finally, an argumentation strategy for apologists. I will conclude in chapter 7.

My hope is to provide insights into these important subjects, for this topic will force consideration of God and his communication, our own human nature, its character and failings, and, as a result, our need for the great salvation in Jesus Christ. It is time, then, to consider the potential unification of the notions of general revelation and natural law.

# Chapter 2

# Unifying the Concepts of General Revelation and Natural Law

The intention of this chapter is first to give a brief historical survey of the concepts of general revelation and natural law. Then it will be considered whether Martin Luther's concept of "legal knowledge" points the way forward to profitably unifying the two concepts. Finally, a critique of modern scholarship in apologetic method will be given, drawing on key themes discussed earlier in the chapter.

## GENERAL REVELATION

General revelation has been a popular post-Reformation term used to denote *truths about God that can be known through nature*. A common distinction has long been made between such general revelation and special revelation, a distinction which helps to clarify the meaning of both terms. The distinction rests in the particularity of special revelation—it is God's message given to particular people at particular times, rather than to all people in all times, as is the case with general revelation.

    The earliest example of this distinction of which I am aware rests with Aquinas. He proposed this distinction in his commentary on Psalm 19 when he contrasted "general" and "special" instruction from God: "Above," in Psalm 19:1–6, ". . . the psalmist spoke of his general instruction, which comes by way of creatures; now," in Psalm 19: 7–14, ". . . he speaks of the special instruction which comes by way of legislation."[1]

While the terminological distinction between a "special" and "general" instruction of God may have originated with Aquinas, it was Calvin's treatment of the conceptual distinction which has had enduring influence in Protestant theology in particular. We may take as representative of Calvin the expression given to this distinction in Article 2 of the Belgic Confession, even though the terms "general" and "special" revelation are not used:

> We know Him by two means: First, by the creation, preservation, and government of the universe; which is before our eyes as a most elegant book, wherein all creatures, great and small, are as so many characters leading us to see clearly the invisible things of God, even his everlasting power and divinity, as the apostle Paul says in Romans 1:20. All which things are sufficient to convince men and leave them without excuse. Second, He makes Himself more clearly and fully known to us by His holy and divine Word, that is to say, as far as is necessary for us to know in this life, to His glory and our salvation.[2]

As Gerrish points out, it is not until the seventeenth-century Protestant Scholastics that the distinction in concept described here is routinely labelled with the terms "general" and "special" revelation.[3] But it should be noted from this quotation that the dominant use of the term "general revelation" comes via reflection on Romans 1:20.[4] The term "general revelation" has regard to God's revelation of himself, to all people, not in such fashion as to allow for their salvation from sin, but in such fashion as to leave them without excuse for rejecting him. We shall have occasion shortly to question the way this definition is limited in scope in that it depicts only God's revelation of himself, rather than a broader ethical ambit. But the distinction between the general and special ambit of God's revelation, as depicted in the terms "general" and "special" revelation, has good biblical grounds for finding favor.

An important element of Calvin's presentation of general revelation was his notion of the sense of the divine, or *sensus divinitatis*. He writes,

---

1. Aquinas, "Commentary on Psalm 18." Note that his commentary on Psalm 18 is a commentary on what is today most commonly referred to as Psalm 19.

2. Schaff, 'The Belgic Confession," 3:384, article 2.

3. Gerrish, "Errors and Insights," 66.

4. Acts 17:22–31 is also often discussed in considering the notion of "general theology."

That there exists in the human mind and indeed by natural instinct, some sense of Deity [*sensus divinitatis*], we hold to be beyond dispute, since God himself, to prevent any man from pretending ignorance, has endued all men with some idea of his Godhead . . . this is not a doctrine which is first learned at school, but one as to which every man is, from the womb, his own master; one which nature herself allows no individual to forget.[5]

Yet while this aspect of Calvin's teaching is well known, the concept of general revelation does not depend on it. For God could, at least in theory, communicate truths about himself to his created beings without doing so through a special sense of the Divine. It will be our contention that he in fact does so. Notice then that my definition of general revelation—truths about God that can be known through nature—does not imply that all people know these truths about God, either through a *sensus divinitatis* or otherwise. For it is my contention that people do not all know the truths about God which he reveals through creation. Indeed, one way of understanding the main thrust of this present work is as a defense of Paul's notion of "no excuse" in Romans 1:20 *without embracing the sensus divinitatis.*

## NATURAL LAW

By "natural law" I mean "truths about ethical universals that can be known through nature." In order to give a sense of how this concept has come down to us, I will briefly survey Thomas Aquinas's and John Calvin's approaches to the subject, paying some attention to their similarities and differences. These two have good claims to be the most enduring influences in this area, in part because of the influence of their overall theological contribution[6]

In his *Summa Theologica*, Aquinas defines four different kinds of law: eternal, natural, human, and divine.[7] Eternal law is "the type of Divine Wisdom, as directing all actions and movements." That is, for Aquinas, eternal law equates with divine reason, through which God rules the universe, "imprinting principles of proper action on all creatures."[8]

Natural law is related: "The light of natural reason, whereby we discern what is good and what is evil, which is the function of the natural law, is

---

5. Calvin, *Institutes*, I.iii.1.

6. The discussion to follow draws especially on the excellent survey work of David VanDrunen: VanDrunen, *Natural Law*, 43–47, 99–107.

7. Aquinas, *Summa Theologica*, I–II q. 90, a. 4.

8. VanDrunen, *Natural Law*, 43.

nothing else than an imprint on us of the Divine Light."[9] Or put another way, natural law is "the rational creature's participation of the eternal law."[10]

Turning to Calvin, his commentary on Romans 2 is a good place to start in understanding his depiction of natural law. There he outlines a natural "implanting" and "imprinting" of the law of God on the human heart.[11] In his *Institutes*, he writes that the internal law, which consists of the commands of the Decalogue, is "written and stamped on every heart."[12] This conception of natural law notably claims that every human heart has in some sense received each element of the law, even if it is marred by sin. Just as I will question the reality of a *sensus divinitatis*, I will also challenge this claim of universal reception of natural law.

David VanDrunen points to divergent teaching on the role of conscience as one important means to distinguish Calvin's doctrine of natural law from that of Aquinas:

> Whereas Thomas spoke of conscience as reason's application of general precepts to particular moral acts, Calvin (more resembling Luther) speaks of conscience as awareness of God's law and judgment. Though Calvin associates conscience with the intellect, he does not describe it as movement from premises to conclusions, but as bringing an immediate awareness of the requirements of natural law. Thomas on the other hand, made the connection between natural law and conscience indirect. He viewed conscience in terms of reasoning from premises to conclusions and therefore also thought that human laws and virtues are known not immediately by natural law but by deduction from its first principles.[13]

This direct reception of natural law is an element in Calvin and many Reformers that I embrace, as will be seen below. Samuel Hopkins later helpfully described such a manner of reception of natural law as "short and easy," a phrase to which I shall return as a neat statement of this key difference.[14]

VanDrunen underlines another key difference between the positions of Calvin and Aquinas on natural law in terms of the way the varying treatment of "nature" and "grace" leads to varying emphases on the impact of sin. His summary is worth quoting at length:

9. Aquinas, *Summa Theologica*, I–II q. 91, a. 2.
10. Aquinas, *Summa Theologica*, I–II q. 91, a. 2.
11. Calvin, *Commentary*.
12. Calvin, *Institutes*, II.iix.1.
13. VanDrunen, *Natural Law*, 101.
14. Hopkins, *Works*, 33.

> Thomas follows Aristotle in identifying the four cardinal virtues. He claims they are attainable by human beings' natural powers alone.... But he modifies Aristotle's account by positing three supernatural or theological virtues as well: faith, hope and love. No one can attain these by the powers of nature but only by the infusion of supernatural grace.... These ideas ... govern Thomas's account of the need for divine revelation. Thomas held that natural law, known by reason, can guide people only to an end proportionate to their natural faculties, whereas divine law, supernaturally revealed by grace, is necessary to guide people to a supernatural, heavenly end.... For Thomas, the fundamental reason why grace is needed in addition to nature is not corruption of nature due to the fall into sin, but the inherent limits of nature itself....
>
> There are several points at which Calvin's thought stands in some tension with Thomas's nature-grace structure.... First, Calvin's assessments of the (non-Christian) philosophers ... tend to be negative.... Furthermore ... in expositing his very stark view of the effects of sin, he asserts that reason, though not entirely taken away, is a corrupted and shapeless ruin.... Also different are Calvin's rationales for the necessity of supernatural revelation ... human sin rather than the limits of human nature is the principal reason why supernatural revelation is necessary.[15]

The concept of natural law that I will be proposing is much more like Calvin's depiction than Aquinas's. I side with Calvin particularly so in these three areas of tension identified by VanDrunen, namely the assessment of non-Christian philosophers, the corruption of reason, and viewing sin as the principal reason for the necessity of special revelation.

## LUTHER'S PATH TOWARDS UNIFYING THE CONCEPTS

Recall that the main question of the present work is as follows: if neither God's universal self-revelation nor truths about ethical universals are reliably accessible through nature, how can God justly judge people for failing to worship him and keep his law, when they are ignorant? A significant element of my answer to the question comes in simplifying it by treating general revelation and natural law as a single entity. My claim is that an important move in the direction of such unification can be found in Luther's

---

15. VanDrunen, *Natural Law*, 106–7.

use of the distinction between "legal knowledge" and "evangelical knowledge," as now shall be outlined.

Luther presents a principle in his Galatians commentary that there is a twofold knowledge of God: there is a general knowledge on the one hand, and a particular knowledge on the other hand. He writes that "all men have the general knowledge, namely that God is, that He has created heaven and earth, that He is just, that He punishes the wicked, etc. . . . The particular, saving knowledge of God comes through the gospel of Christ."[16] In his eleventh sermon on John 1, Luther uses different language for the same distinction, distinguishing between a condemning "legal knowledge" and a saving "evangelical knowledge."[17]

Luther makes this distinction while expounding John 1:18. The context is that he is discussing how one might harmonize the saying that "no one has ever seen God" with Jesus' declaration that "if the Son . . . had not come to reveal God to us, no one would know Him."[18] He declares that the answer comes in seeing that there are

> two kinds of knowledge of God: the one is the knowledge of the Law; the other is the knowledge of the Gospel. . . . Although the same truth was stated still more clearly by Moses, it still remains true that all rational beings can of themselves determine that it is wrong to disobey father and mother and the government, to murder, commit adultery, steal, curse, and blaspheme. . . . Reason can arrive at a "legal knowledge" of God.[19]

The contrast with "evangelical knowledge" is expressed as follows:

> The other sort of knowledge of God emerges from the Gospel. There we learn that all the world is by nature an abomination before God, subject to God's wrath and the devil's power, and is eternally damned. From this the world could not extricate itself except through God's Son. . . . He became man, died and rose again, . . . extinguishing sin, death and the devil. . . . This is the true and thorough knowledge and way of thinking about God; it is called the knowledge of grace and truth, the "evangelical knowledge" of God.[20]

---

16. Luther, *Luther's Works*, 26.399.
17. Luther, *Luther's Works*, 22.151–52.
18. John 8:54–55. Luther, *Luther's Works*, 22.150.
19. Luther, *Luther's Works*, 22.150–51.
20. Luther, *Luther's Works*, 22.152.

Luther's description and distinction here has many strengths. In it, he has laid down a pathway upon which one can run further than Luther himself saw, especially utilizing his terms "legal" and "evangelical." It is true that much has been made of Luther's law/grace distinction, but not in the direction here intended. For implicit in his term "legal knowledge" is that there is sufficient knowledge given by God for legal condemnation of all who do not respond. The term thus reflects more than just that the knowledge is communicated generally to all, as is reflected in the term "general revelation." "Legal knowledge" also indicates that the result of God's communication is that all people have sufficient knowledge available to them, that they have no excuse before the legal court of God's final justice. The contrast with "evangelical knowledge" is that it is saving in nature rather than condemning. Evangelical knowledge is also limited in its dissemination, which forms another neat contrast with "legal knowledge." As such the legal/evangelical distinction is one that improves on other dualisms such as general/special revelation or Aquinas's faith/reason dualism, for it better depicts the distinction in reality between universally communicated legal truths and locally communicated gospel truths.

Yet two weaknesses remain in Luther's formulation. First, because Luther's distinction was written in reflection on knowing *God*, he does not use it to its full potential. He could have run further down the pathway than he did. For one does well to conceive of a "legal knowledge" which refers to all knowledge required to live a righteous life under the covenant of works.[21] Such "legal knowledge" is more expansive than in Luther's discussion of legal knowledge since it includes an array of moral knowledge. For example, included under this wider concept of "legal knowledge" is knowledge that "You should not steal," that "there are possessions,"[22] as well as "You should worship God" and "God is creator." In this way, one can see that Luther's

---

21. The terms "covenant of works" and "covenant of grace" are terms commonly used in Reformed theology, although the full assumption-set often accompanying those terms is not intended here. All that is intended is to say that God has revealed his moral requirements of all people, that he has done so through nature, and these requirements can be described as "the requirements of the covenant of works." The covenant of works is such that if a person obeys them perfectly, he will live (Lev 18:5; Matt 19:17; Luke 10:28). This contrasts with the covenant of grace, wherein the requirements for eternal life are repentance and faith in Jesus. For one discussion of these covenants, see Bavinck, *Sin and Salvation*, 224–28.

22. "That there are possessions" is a statement of moral knowledge, since it is an essential point for a person to believe if they are to believe that they should not steal. Likewise, "That there is a God" is a statement of moral knowledge, since it is an essential point for a person to believe if they are to believe that they should worship him.

dualism of "legal knowledge" and "evangelical knowledge" provides headings to incorporate both natural law and knowledge of God.

A second weakness in Luther's distinction is that he understands "legal knowledge" to be completely subjectively received by all rather than simply being an objective communication by God to all, received imperfectly by sinful people. This subjective rendering could not be sustained, as later theologians wrestled with the reality that not all people outwardly acknowledged the legal knowledge that Luther insisted that they subjectively possessed. So in time, theologians placed less emphasis on the legal/evangelical knowledge distinction as they sought to *demonstrate* all the kinds of knowledge, both evangelical and legal, that many were subjectively denying. As such, Luther would have been better served distinguishing evangelical and legal revelation, rather than evangelical and legal knowledge.

I will use this distinction, then, in what follows. "Legal revelation" becomes my preferred term to describe "expanded general revelation," or the "unified concept of general revelation and natural law." So "legal revelation" is "the expressible communication of God to all, communicating that which humanity needs to live a righteous life under the covenant of works." "Evangelical revelation" becomes my preferred term to replace "special revelation," namely "the expressible communication of God, communicating that which humanity needs to live a righteous life under the covenant of grace."

The advantages of this change are twofold: First, this new set of terms includes the "ethical" as well as the "theological" in consideration of that which God communicates generally. This is important if one wants to depict the entirety of that which God reveals generally which is also relevant to every person's culpability before him. Second, the terms "legal" and "evangelical" depict the content of God's communication, whereas "general" and "special" depict only the scope of God's communication. The former is more important, and moreover, the theological claim being made here is that the former implies the latter. For the theological claim underlying this change in terminology is that God has chosen to reveal, generally, all that people need to know to be without excuse, legally, before his throne of judgment. Thus in replacing "general" with "legal," I have not ceased to describe that which God communicates generally, but rather have stated the content of that which he does communicate generally. So the replacement terms bring additional theological depth by resting on important claims. But a key reason that Luther stated his distinction in terms of knowledge rather than revelation, as *subjective* rather than *objective* knowledge, was his misreading of Romans 1:20. Luther's admittedly common misreading of that section of Scripture held Paul to teach that every human has a knowledge of God.

In fact, as we shall argue, Romans 1 need not be read that way, and is best not read that way. Luther also overstates the case when he says that the gentiles are *all* aware that murder, adultery, theft, cursing, lying, deceit, and blasphemy are wrong.[23] Neither Romans 1 nor Romans 2 can be pressed to make claims that bold. Yet Luther is considerably closer to the mark here than Aquinas, for Luther's treatment of legal knowledge as an inescapable deliverance of man's conscience, enables him to rightly treat both the moral law and conscience in their functions of condemning the sinner and leaving him without excuse. Moreover, Luther is right to derive from Scripture the reality of a general knowledge of God. This concept is best understood, though, differently from Luther, as a knowledge of God which is attained by *some but not all* people, from what God has made.

## APPLYING THE TERMINOLOGY: THE QUESTION OF APOLOGETIC METHOD

Some of the benefits of this notion of "legal revelation" can be seen in considering apologetic method. In what follows, I will briefly outline the context of the debate about apologetic method before using our new terminology to provide an assessment of that debate.

With the increasing influence of the Enlightenment in the sixteenth century and beyond, it became more common for theologians to seek to *demonstrate* the truths of Christianity to a potentially doubting audience. Many presented philosophical arguments for God's existence and character, in various forms. For example, Johnathan Edwards argued in favor of God's existence and power by asking about the reason for the movement of the planets.[24] In his interpretation of Romans 1:20, he saw an implied support for a "doctrine of necessity" playing its part in a "proof of the being of God."[25] Richard Baxter wrote a six-hundred-page work, *The Reasons of the Christian Religion*, with appeal to evidences in favor of Christianity. In this way the Puritans contributed to a long Protestant trend of treating together, arguments for any and every contested element of the Christian faith.

The problem is that matters which are at heart ethical questions such as "Is there a God?" were treated as though they were the same kind of question as those which are at heart historical questions, such as "Did Jesus die on a cross outside Jerusalem?" That is, both were taken simply as Christian claims for which reasons should be given. Yet it should be plain that ethical

23. Luther, *Luther's Works*, 22.149.
24. Edwards, "Miscellanies," 75.
25. Edwards, *Power of God*, 12.

questions require a very different approach epistemically from historical questions. This latter point would no doubt be accepted by all those like Baxter who wrote such "reasons for belief"-style works. But the point they missed was that the truth of God's existence is an ethical question, falling under my category of "legal revelation," because at the Last Judgment before God, all people will be blameworthy for not responding to God as they should, just as they will be blameworthy for the times they stole, or lied, or committed sexual sin. Such "legal revelation" objectively presses against us all, whether or not we subjectively receive it. That is why we will have no excuse on the Last Day for not knowing it. Such revelation must therefore be treated differently from historical aspects of the Christian gospel, like Jesus' death outside Jerusalem, which sits under the category I have described as "evangelical revelation." For of course, no one can be blamed for not knowing about Jesus' death if they have never had a chance to hear about Jesus. But they can be blamed for not knowing that they should give God thanks, or that they should not steal. Lack of awareness of this distinction and its implications can be seen in many modern works on the subject of apologetic method.

One representative example is that of Douglas Groothius. In setting forth his "cumulative and winsome approach" to apologetics, Groothius both outlines and critiques the "apologetic systems" of Fideism, Presuppositionalism, Reformed Epistemology, and Evidentialism.[26] As he does so, he understands these various schools to be promoting *one overall method of apologetic argument*, with no mention of whether or how objections from an interlocutor regarding ethics might be treated differently from those regarding history. Just as these apologetics schools do not consider treating ethics differently methodologically, neither does Groothius. So in opposing Fideism, Groothius argues that the "Christian worldview" is not exempt from logic.[27] This point is well made, but does not consider whether some subset of the Christian worldview, such as "legal revelation," might be exempt from his sweeping statement, or whether it might require different treatment methodologically. Similarly, in opposing Presuppositionalism, Groothius argues that good reasoning is not "autonomous" or "apostate."[28] Without ruling on the merits of his argument, one can observe that he is speaking about reasoning in general at this point. He does not consider whether reasoning ought to look different in certain subsets of the Christian truth claims, such as within ethical as opposed to historical knowledge.

26. Groothius, *Christian Apologetics*, 60–70.
27. Groothius, *Christian Apologetics*, 61.
28. Groothius, *Christian Apologetics*, 63.

He makes no distinction between reasoning towards ethical conclusions and other conclusions. Groothius critiques Reformed Epistemology on the grounds that it is too limited. For while a person may be able to "defeat defeaters" aimed at Christian faith, "what if he or she questions God's very existence or the authenticity of the Scriptures?"[29] Groothius's point is that Plantinga's Reformed Epistemology does not give enough to say to such a person. The critical point though is that even here, where different kinds of objections to Christian faith are briefly considered, Groothius never considers whether *ethical questions* as a set, or more precisely, "legal revelation," should be treated differently from other questions. Lastly, Groothius objects to Evidentialism by underscoring that "more apologetic reasoning may be required than simply establishing historical facts."[30] This is a well-made point, but the additional reasoning Groothius has in mind is the use of natural theological arguments for God's existence. He is not contemplating whether contested biblical claims of an historical nature, such as those typical within "evangelical revelation," might need a different methodology from those of an *ethical nature*, such as those within the category of "legal revelation."

Groothius is typical, being one of many apologetic writers who do not consider whether, methodologically, the matters of ethics should be treated differently from matters of history. Other examples are Cowan,[31] Morley,[32] Boa,[33] Dulles,[34] Craig,[35] and Taylor.[36] Hence imprecisely defined concepts

---

29. Groothius, *Christian Apologetics*, 67–68.
30. Groothius, *Christian Apologetics*, 70.
31. See Cowan, "Five Views on Apologetics," 15–20.

32. Morley gives a neat chart of ten different apologetic approaches. The closest of these to an approach that treats ethical matters distinctly from others is Hanna's veridicalism, for whom God's existence is one of a number of "givens." This is still a good distance away from a distinct consideration of ethical matters within an apologetic approach. See Morley, *Mapping Apologetics*, 14–15; Hanna, *Crucial Questions*.

33. Boa, *Faith Has Its Reasons*, 34–36.
34. Dulles, *History of Apologetics*, 353–58.

35. Craig cites 1 Pet 3:15 as evidence for his point that responding to questions and objections is *commanded*. Craig describes this necessary extra step beyond preaching as the need to "show" Christianity to be true, embracing the need to "reason with an unbeliever," using "arguments," and using "rational argumentation." He states this as a general principle for all potential questions, thereby ignoring the question of whether ethical questions might need fundamentally different handling. See Craig, *Reasonable Faith*, 56–57.

36. Taylor is similar to Craig in his use of 1 Pet 3:15. See Taylor, *Introducing Apologetics*, 19–32.

of God's revelation remain to this day and yield a discourse in theology and apologetics which is not as gospel-shaped as it should be.

## CONCLUSION

In conclusion, I have focused in this chapter on the character of general revelation and natural law. Four points should be especially noted.

First, I proposed definitions and sketched a history of the concepts of general revelation and natural law, proposing a definition of each concept that does not entail a subjective reception of particular content by all people. That is, I have proposed a definition of general revelation which does not entail the existence of a *sensus divinitatis*. Similarly, I have proposed a definition of natural law that does not imply that the entire law of God is written in every person's heart. I shall be arguing below that such understandings are not necessary for people to be held culpable before God.

Second, I argued that there is a benefit to be derived from unifying the concepts of general revelation and natural law, into a single concept of "legal revelation." I defined "legal revelation" as "the expressible communication of God to all, communicating that which humanity needs to live a righteous life under the covenant of works." I contrasted this with "evangelical revelation," defined as "the expressible communication of God, communicating that which humanity needs to live a righteous life under the covenant of grace." I argued that Luther walked some of the path towards this united concept. I also argued that the distinction between legal revelation and evangelical revelation is superior to other dualities such the general/special revelation distinction or the faith/reason distinction. This new terminology has the advantage of considering *both* the "theological" and the "ethical" as part of that which God communicates generally, without indicating that this revelation is subjectively received by all. It also has the strength of incorporating the theological claim that God communicates generally that which all need, to live under the covenant of works. For the term "legal" denotes this key function of that revelation, that a law is given, sufficient for us to adjudicate, and therefore sufficient for God to condemn our moral failure. Correspondingly, the term "evangelical" denotes a key function of that revelation, that a gospel is given, sufficient to save. Note that like the distinction between "general" and "special" revelation, there is overlap between the categories of "legal" and "evangelical" revelation, for the ethical is also part of the revealed gospel.

Third, I critiqued the post-Enlightenment emphasis of providing reasons for all Christian claims, including ethical claims alongside historical claims without a clear distinction between the two. The implied false assumption was that ethical revelation, which objectively presses on us all, is the same kind of thing as historical revelation, which does not. I showed that this is an endemic blind spot in modern apologetic scholarship.

Fourth, I showed that this distinction aids in the answering of the main question of this present work, in that it simplifies. The major question addressed by this present work is as follows: if neither general revelation nor natural law are accessible to people reliably, how can God justly judge them for their ignorance and hold them morally culpable for failing to live according to revelation they cannot reliably access? In combining general revelation and natural law into one concept, we have turned a question about two concepts into a question about just one concept, thus simplifying the task.

My next step will be a discussion of Romans 1 and 2. I will first state some additional key propositions for answering the book's major question. Then I shall journey through Romans 1 and 2 to see if these propositions are viable in the face of a careful reading.

# Chapter 3

## Testing Propositions against the Text of Romans 1 and 2

The point has now been reached where the proposal of this work can be stated as a series of propositions. Having stated these propositions, this chapter will take us on a reading journey through Romans 1 and 2. The aim will not be to demonstrate the propositions from the text, but rather to see if the propositions are viable in the face of a careful reading of these key chapters.

The problem is, if neither general revelation nor natural law are accessible to people reliably, how can God justly judge them for their ignorance and hold them morally culpable for failing to live according to revelation they cannot reliably access?

In asking this question, I mean by "general revelation" truths about God that can be known through nature, especially as described in 1:19–20. By "natural law" I mean truths about ethical universals that can be known through nature, especially as described in 2:14–15. The argument that follows is organized as a pair of propositions with sub-propositions attached.

*The first proposition is that the notions of general revelation and natural law are best treated together as a single unit in posing this problem and answering it.* This is because they seem so to overlap with each other that no firm line can be drawn between them, and because their union seems to constitute a set of truths with an important function, the truths according to which all humanity will be judged under the covenant of works. Hence chapter 2 proposed the new terminology of "legal revelation," being "the expressible communication of God to all, communicating that which humanity needs to live a righteous life under the covenant of works." So the proposition is that the notions of general revelation and natural law can be treated together as this "legal revelation." This union of concepts aids us in addressing this problem because it simplifies, turning a question about two notions into a question about only one notion.

The second proposition is that the broadest answer to the problem is "it is humanity's fault not God's that legal revelation does not get through to people reliably." I suggest five realities that point to it being humanity's fault rather than God's:

i. *Each element of legal revelation's content is designed for "short and easy"[1] reception*, so that it is not God's fault for making legal revelation too complicated or difficult to receive. It is not too complicated or difficult to receive.

ii. *Each element of legal revelation is communicated universally and continually,* so that God cannot be accused of making it only available in certain localized times or places. This is saying that a part of my definition of "legal revelation," namely its universality, is a key reality in defending God against the charge that he condemns unjustly.

iii. *All people internalize an ethical map approximating legal revelation, but we do so with flaws*—flaws that are culpable, with blame resting upon us as individuals, and others who have influenced us, but not with God.

iv. *Problems in humanity's disposition, which hinder the reception of legal revelation, are humanity's fault*, since Adam and Eve could wholly receive it pre-fall. While the third reality blames us for our flawed *internalization* of legal revelation, this fourth reality blames humanity for our fallen *nature* which cannot internalize legal revelation reliably. This endemic inability is God's just judgment on us for Adam's sin and for our other forebears' sin and for our individual sin.

v. *God's continued communication of his legal revelation is manifest*, seen in the fact that each element of legal revelation is still being received through nature by many people, pointing to the blame resting on us, rather than God, for his revelation not being reliably received.

---

1. Recall from chapter 2 that the phrase "short and easy" was taken from Samuel Hopkins. "Immediate and accessible" is a potential alternative expression.

It should be clear that if these propositions hold, these are good answers to this book's major problem. The claim is not that these are the only answers, but that they are good answers. With these propositions briefly outlined, I now turn to provide a fresh reading of Romans 1 and 2. Paul's statement in 1:19–20 refers to the knowledge of God from creation, whereas 2:14–15 refers to the divine law written in the heart. The first passage is key in historical discussion of general revelation, and the second is key in historical discussion of natural law—the two elements I am proposing to combine into the notion of "legal revelation."

It is not original to consider 1:19–20 and 2:15 together. Melanchthon for example drew a parallel between these two passages in his early writing, stating explicitly that a view of inborn knowledge of God underlies the thinking of both, with this concept of inborn knowledge sourced in Cicero.[2] Pannenberg critiques Melanchthon's reading of 1:19–20, saying, "A difficulty for this view for Melanchthon was that the knowledge of God in 1:19–20 is obviously associated with experience of the world . . . the knowledge of 1:20 is not innate, like that of 2:15, but acquired."[3] Pannenberg raises an important issue when he asks whether the mechanisms described in Romans 1 and 2 are parallel. If they are parallel, then it is possible that general revelation and natural law can be folded together in the form of a "legal revelation" that we are describing. But if Pannenberg is correct, such that Romans 2 describes an "innate" knowledge, but Romans 1 does not, then such a folding together of general revelation and natural law seems impossible. The present proposal is that general revelation and natural law are, in fact, one phenomenon with two overlapping aspects discernible in two overlapping spheres of human moral experience—our experience of God, and our experience of God's creation.

Note that in what follows, an exegesis of Romans 1 and 2 will be undertaken that is consistent with there being a parallel mechanism behind 1:19–20 and 2:14–15. But the mechanism is not, as with Melanchthon, that the truths of general revelation and natural law are inborn in all. It is a reading that sees both mechanisms consistent with proposals labelled (i)–(v) above, which is a model of "internalization" of revelation, rather than of inborn knowledge.

I will spend more time in Romans 1 than in Romans 2, since original claims about Romans 1 require some detailed defense. All of 1:18—2:1 will be exegeted, as well as 2:14–15. Space will be devoted to considering whether 1:21–32 is an historical narrative because the answer bears on the

---

2. Pauck, *Melanchthon*, 51.
3. Pannenberg, *Systematic Theology*, 109, 117.

universality of key claims in that section. Time will also be spent considering the question, "For what is humanity without excuse?" because the answer gives insight into the source of human disposition to misread God's legal revelation.

## EXEGESIS OF ROMANS 1:8—2:1 AND 2:14-15

> [18] the wrath of God is being revealed from heaven against all the godlessness and wickedness of people who suppress the truth by their wickedness,

The context of 1:18—2:1 is that Paul has just given the thematic statement of the letter (1:16-17).[4] With the introductory section of the epistle concluded, he is now ready to make a lengthy exposition of the content of his gospel. He begins by speaking of God's wrath being revealed from heaven. But who are the subjects of the passage and therefore also the subjects of this wrath?

Traditionally, 1:18-32 has been understood to be exclusively about the gentiles.[5] The idea is that Paul first talks about gentiles, and then moves on to Jews in chapter 2, so that he can reach the conclusion that "Jews and Gentiles alike are held to be under sin."[6] Arguments in favor of a gentile referent include first that the knowledge of God described in 1:18-32 comes from natural revelation alone, and second, that "the passage is reminiscent of Jewish apologetic arguments in which Gentile idolatry was derided."[7]

However, recent scholarship has moved away from this Gentile (Rom 1:18-32)/Jew (Rom 2) division. The reasons for the change include (i) the word "Gentiles" is not used in 1:18-32, but the word "people" is; (ii) the turn to idolatry in 1:21-31 uses language reminiscent of the fall (Gen 3) and golden calf (Exod 32) incidents, so that Jews may also be in view; (iii) the connection between 1:32 and 2:1 makes better sense if the people spoken to in chapter 2 are included in 1:32; the latter includes Jews, so also the former.

---

4. Romans 1:16-17 is the thematic statement of the letter. See Cranfield, *Romans*, 87-102; Dunn, *Romans 1-8*, 37; Fitzmyer, *Romans*, 98; Jewett, *Romans*, vii; Moo, *Romans*, 63-79.

5. Those who take the view that 1:18-32 has *at least an emphasis* on gentiles while chapter 2 focuses on Jews include Luther, *Commentary on Romans*, 42, 51; Sanday and Headlam, *Romans*, 39, 53; Hendriksen, *Romans*, 67, 86; Morris, *Romans*, 73, 107; Fitzmyer, *Romans*, 269, 296; Osborne, *Romans*, 45, 59; Schreiner, *Romans*, 81, 102; Kruse, *Romans*, 82, 117.

6. Rom 3:9.

7. Moo, *Romans*, 97. See also Wis 13.

This new consensus has much to commend it and is compelling. Note that writers such as Hooker and Levison contend that Adam is in view in 1:19–32. Hooker argues against the view of H. Owen that Romans 1 teaches "every idolater, at some time, has a measure of insight into God's θειότης and ... suppresses it." She contends instead that 1:19–32 is speaking of humanity's sin in relation to the Genesis creation and fall accounts. So for Hooker, God made himself supremely plain to Adam,[8] Adam was without excuse,[9] Adam claimed to be wise but became a fool,[10] and Adam gave his allegiance to a creature, the serpent, rather than to the Creator.[11] Hooker does not mean that Adam is *solely* in view here. But she is an important example, heavily cited, of the view that Adam is, in part, the referent in 1:19–32.[12] My contention, to be argued below, is that the referent throughout is best expressed as "all humanity," with the present tense of 1:19–20 showing that modern humanity, and not just Adam, are in view in those two verses. My contention is also that 1:21 commences an historical narrative about humanity, one that begins with Adam, as will also be argued in detail below.

So both Jews and Gentiles are in view in 1:18–32—"all humanity." However this does not mean "all people without exception," nor is it completely uniform through the argument, as will also be discussed shortly. God's wrath then is directed at humanity as a whole, and it is directed against humanity's godlessness and wickedness.[13] The discussion and argument that follows therefore concerns humanity's moral failure and whether humanity might have an excuse for it.[14]

> [19] since what may be known about God is plain to them,[15] because God has made it plain to them. [20] For since the creation

---

8. Rom 1:19.

9. Rom 1:20.

10. Rom 1:21.

11. Rom 1:25.

12. See Hooker, "Adam in Romans i"; Levison, "Adam and Eve," 519–34; Dunn, *Romans 1–8*, 53; Owen, "Scope," 141.

13. Cranfield is likely correct when he writes that ἀσέβεια characterizes sin as "an attack on the majesty of God," while ἀδικία describes it as "a violation of God's just order." See Cranfield, *Romans*, 112.

14. For more on the question "Without excuse for what moral failure?" see the excursus below.

15. The phrase ἐν αὐτοῖς translated "to them" by the NIV is probably better rendered "in their midst": "In their midst and all around them and also in their own creaturely existence ... God is objectively manifest." Godet and Meyer take this revelation to occur subjectively within each person's conscience, with the latter referring to Paul's mention of "conscience" and "heart" in 2:15 in so doing. But as Cranfield points out, such an understanding of ἐν αὐτοῖς is incompatible with v. 21. See Cranfield, *Romans*,

of the world God's invisible qualities—his eternal power and divine nature—have been clearly seen, being understood from what has been made, so that people are without excuse.

These phrases build logically on the previous verse. God's wrath is being revealed against the godlessness and wickedness of humanity (1:18) because it is wicked that they do not know what God has made plain. The fact that God has made things *plain* (φανερός) implies that each person, at least each person who has avoided severe handicap as they have grown, ought to know these things. It is their plainness, which means that both humanity as a block, and each individual, are without excuse for not knowing them. This plainness implies a "short and easy" mode of reception, for otherwise the excuse might be forthcoming by some that these truths were too "complicated and difficult" for them to understand.

The phrase τὸ γνωστὸν τοῦ θεοῦ, "what may be known about God," is broad in scope, in that it includes both knowledge about God *and* knowledge of ethics relating to God.[16] The fact that ethics relating to God are in view can be seen in 1:21, for the logical connectives between 1:19 and 1:21 indicate that "what may be known about God" (1:19) should lead people to glorify God and give him thanks (1:21). It is not just that people should understand some of God's characteristics—his eternal power and divine nature—through what he has made, it is also that they should know their obligation to glorify him and give him thanks, but this in turn implies a substantial scope of ethical reality that people should know in this fashion. Paul may be envisaging a reflex instinct to worship here, but it should not be considered, for that reason, any less an ethical obligation to worship him. For the need to glorify God and give him thanks implies obligations not to commit idolatry,[17] not to live for things or persons other than God, and more. Thus here, general revelation is overlapping with natural law.

Paul's phrase ἀπό κτίσεως κόσμου, "since the creation of the world," is a temporal phrase. This temporal, historical element is introduced to make the point that God has not made himself plain at only one point or only one

---

113–14; Godet, *Romans*, 103; Meyer, *Romans*, 79.

16. Commentators commonly expend energy here discussing whether the passage teaches some kind of natural theology, but spend less or no time considering the ethical content that is captured by this phrase, "what may be known about God." But Paul's point is more than that humanity are without excuse for not believing that God exists or for not understanding his character. His point is that humanity are without excuse for their moral failure to honor and thank God. The ethical should not be neglected here. This is at odds with Dunn, *Romans 1–8*, 56–57. For a discussion more in tune with Paul's argument on this score, see Achtemeier, *Romans*, 36–39.

17. Keener sees this, and titles 1:18–23 "Inexcusable idolatry." Keener, *Romans*, 31.

era of history. If he had done so, many would have missed out on God's self-revelation. Rather, God has revealed himself consistently since the creation of the world, with the result that no one has missed out on God's revelation in "what has been made." Thus no one, from any period in history, has an excuse for their God-ignorance.[18] The fault for the failure is on humanity's side, since we have suppressed the truth, not God's side, since he has made himself consistently plain.

Paul does not explicitly state what "the things he has made" might be, and whether Paul has in mind all the things God has made or just some is not stated. If he refers to only some of the things that God has made, there is no explicit statement as to what the things might be. Owen lists the human self, history, and nature as possible candidates.[19] However, since Paul places no limitation on the extent of things in view, neither will I. It is best to infer that there is a wide range of God's creation that shows God's invisible qualities to all people. Against the early Melanchthon cited above, and with Pannenberg, one should not characterize the knowledge of God, here described, as *only inborn or innate knowledge*. God's revelation has been so sufficiently and consistently plain that, ever since the creation of the world, his invisible qualities have been seen and understood.

Literally τά γάρ ἀόρατα αὐτοῦ / ἀπό κτίσεως κόσμου τοῖς ποιήμασιν νοούμενα καθορᾶται is translated "his invisible things, since the creation of the world, being understood in the things made, have been seen." Both νοούμενα, "being understood," and καθορᾶται, "have been seen," are rendered in the passive voice because the claim is a limited one. Paul is not saying that the typical person over humanity's history has seen and understood God's invisible qualities. Nor is it implied that there exists *an argument* for God's invisible qualities from premises universally accepted.[20] Paul's point, by contrast, is that *some* people, ever since the creation of the world, have seen God's invisible qualities, understanding these qualities in the things God has made. They *have been clearly seen*. This somewhat limited claim is nonetheless still sufficient to yield Paul's conclusion about humanity as a

---

18. The phrase εἰς τὸ εἶναι αὐτοὺς ἀναπολογήτους is best translated "so that they are without excuse," or "with the result that they are without excuse," not "in order that they might be without excuse." See Wallace, *Greek Grammar*, 592–94.

19. Augustine supposed the reference to be to the human self. See Owen, "Scope," 134.

20. That such an argument for God's existence might exist is not a necessary conclusion for the exegesis that follows—indeed, if an argument of any difficulty were necessarily involved in concluding that God has certain qualities, one would think many would have an excuse for not knowing—namely that the argument was too difficult for them to grasp.

whole, "they are without excuse."[21] Since at least some people have clearly seen God's qualities, throughout history, ever since the time of Adam and Eve, the excuse cannot be made that it is impossible to understand God's self-revelation.

Moo holds an unnecessary assumption when he writes the following regarding 1:20:

> [Paul] asserts that people actually come to "understand" something about God's existence and nature. How universal is this perception? The flow of Paul's argument makes any limitation impossible. Those who perceive the attributes of God in creation must be the same as those who suppress the truth in unrighteousness and are therefore liable to the wrath of God. Paul makes clear that this includes all people (see 3:9, 19–20).[22]

For Moo, every individual perceives the attributes of God in creation, then suppresses this truth, and therefore is liable to the wrath of God. But in reasoning this way, Moo is making unsubstantiated assertions beyond the thrust of the text.

For in fact, 1:20 merely says that God's invisible qualities "have been understood." This is still enough to render all people without excuse, on the logic that "if so many people understood from creation alone, *you should have understood too.*" That is, this Pauline phrase could mean "understood by various people at various points in time in various places," rather than "understood necessarily by all people everywhere." So this is plausibly an argument by Paul that the whole of humanity is guilty by the precedent of the insight of some. That some can acknowledge God, discerning his power and nature from creation alone, means that those who do not, have no excuse.

It is the failure to find this logic that leads Moo in his chosen direction. Yet his understanding necessitates a strained position when it comes to interpreting the experience of lifelong atheists who state that they have never understood God's qualities. Moo's reading implies that either such atheists are lying, or that they are self-deceived regarding their own understanding of God. While self-deception is a real phenomenon, there is a real plausibility problem in concluding that people really understand what they declare they have never understood. A subconscious "understanding," denied by the conscious self, and never experienced by the conscious self, is a strange kind of "understanding" indeed.

---

21. It is not necessary, nor correct, to say, as Reymond and others do, that this passage teaches that "there is no such thing among humanity as an actual atheist." See Reymond, *Systematic Theology*, 143.

22. See Moo, *Romans*, 105.

But I have shown that this strained approach of Moo and others is unnecessary. For one element of Paul's argument plausibly reduces to *"they understood it so you should have understood it too."* God has made himself clear enough that throughout history men and women saw who he was from his creation alone. This has continued since the creation of the world, underlining the consistency and faithfulness of God's self-revelation, and the continuing possibility of discerning God's nature and power from his creation alone.

A rejoinder might be made at this point by a would-be excuse maker: "God, you didn't make me as intelligent or as well-read as those others who understood you from what you made." But the nature of Paul's conclusion shows that he is not speaking of an understanding that comes through a difficult argument requiring intelligence or wide reading, for, if it did, that excuse would be plausible, whereas Paul himself is insisting that the manner of God's self-revelation leaves people without excuse. The implication then is that the phrase "being understood from what has been made" describes a "short and easy" process of coming to know the truths in question, and not necessarily by deductive reasoning or argument.

The term ἀναπολόγητος, "without excuse," has its origin in a Greek legal and rhetorical context, in particular within speeches of defense.[23] The defense in view here is that of the Last Judgment before God.[24] And this raises the important question which will now be addressed: without excuse for what? Exactly what matter or matters does Paul have in mind for which humanity might want to mount a defense?

---

23. Liddell and Scott, "Ἀναπολογέομαι," 207–8.
24. Jewett, *Romans*, 156.

## EXCURSUS: WITHOUT EXCUSE FOR WHAT?

The structure of Romans 1:18–32[25] can be divided into two parts, 1:18–21 and 1:22–32.[26] The centrality of this concept of "no excuse" is seen in the dual observations that first, 1:18–21 reaches its logical high point[27] in the claim that people are without excuse, and second that 1:22–32 is a parallel argument to 1:18–21, providing further detail for the same claims. Thus one can see the importance of answering the prior question, *without excuse for what?*

In seeking a succinct answer, one might have thought to survey the titles which commentators apply to 1:18–32, since such titles often present each commentator's summary of the human problem as described in 1:18–32.[28] Such a survey turns up terms such as "need," "failure," "sin," "sins," "unrighteousness," and being "accountable." These are imprecise, and quite varied.

---

25. The structure of 1:18–32 is not a settled matter in scholarship. There are many attempts to identify the structure with reference to the repeated use of (μετ) ἤλλαξαν, "they exchanged" (1:23, 25, 26), or παρέδωκεν, "he gave over" (1:24, 26, 28), or διό/ διά τοῦτο, "because" (1:21, 24, 26). It is better to see the structure through identifying 1:22–32 as depicting a history of humanity from Adam to present time, and thus dividing the passage into two sections, 1:18–21, and 1:22–32. The first section then explains that humanity is without excuse, deserving the unfolding of God's wrath upon them. The second section outlines the unfolding history of humanity's descent into sin from Adam to the present day, also outlining God's unfolding wrath against that sin. Examples of scholars advocating structures from threefold use of terms include Klostermann, "Die Adäquate Vergeltung," 1–6; Schulz, "Die Anklage," 161–73; Popkes, "Zum Aufbau und Charakter," 490–501; Bouwman, "Noch Einmal Römer," 411–14. See also Fitzmyer, *Romans*, 276.

26. Verse 21 should be seen as connected with the section before it (1:18–20), not with the section after it. The split between sections is seen in the lack of conjunction—an asyndeton between 1:21 and 1:22. However, the high point of the logic of 1:18–21 comes in verse 20, "so that they are without excuse." Verse 1:21 is connected to 1:20 by the subordinating γὰρ conjunction, διότι, "because." This underlines that the endpoint of the logic was reached in 1:20, and that 1:21 is further explaining that end point.

27. Rom 1:21 is subordinate to 1:20, which reached the high point of its logic with the purpose clause "so that people are without excuse."

28. It has been uncommon for commentators to use the phrase "No excuse" in their summary description of Romans 1:18–32. This has been partly because commentators have often chosen to emphasise the distinction between gentiles and Jews in their titles, and partly because they have also often chosen terms to describe humanity's predicament depicted in these verses, leaving no room to mention the no-excuse theme. In describing humanity's predicament within their titles for 1:18–32, commentators have variously focused on humanity's *need* (Luther, Bruce), *failure* (Sanday and Headlam), *sin* (Murray), *sins* (Kruse), *unrighteousness* (Schreiner), and being *accountable* (Moo). Luther, *Romans*, 42; Sanday and Headlam, *Romans*, 39; Murray, *Romans*, 1:34; Schreiner, *Romans*, 81; Moo, *Romans*, 95; Kruse, *Romans*, 82; Bruce, *Romans*, 77.

In searching for a better answer, observe first that humanity's wicked *deeds* are in view. For throughout 1:18–32, numerous misdeeds are described and attributed to humanity. Yet 1:18–32 does more than simply describe the evil deeds of humanity. Paul himself, looking backward from 3:9, declares what he has already argued: "We have already made the charge that Jews and Gentiles alike are all . . . ὑφ᾽ ἁμαρτίαν, 'under sin.'" This is different from the claim that all have sinned (3:23).[29] While commentators commonly explain the phrase "under sin" in 3:9 as personifying sin in the role of slavemaster,[30] they have little to say about precisely where and how Paul has described this "slavemaster" notion in 1:18—3:8.[31]

Sanders, Räisänen, and Donaldson[32] contest Paul's claim in 3:9, saying that his case is unconvincing, internally inconsistent, and exaggerated. Räisänen points out that the move from "some commit gross sins" to "all are under sin" is "a blatant non sequitur." And it is true that in 1:18–32 the majority have not committed some of the sins mentioned. But in 1:18–32, the focus is not only on the gross sins, but also on the *state of* humanity, including our futile thinking and foolish hearts (1:21). These latter two aspects of the fallen human condition are true of all without exception, and Paul intends to convey particularly this. Sanders thinks that 2:12–15 and 2:26 do not square well with the conclusion of 3:9. But Sanders has not grasped that 1:18–32 does all the work in the argument by charging Jews and Gentiles to

---

29. Jewett is an example of a commentator failing to make the distinction between a charge that all are under sin and that all have sinned. He writes regarding 3:9, "Commentators have wondered exactly where Paul has made the case that all have sinned." Those who have doubted that Paul has done what he claims to have done in 3:9 include Zeller and Räisänen. See Jewett, *Romans*, 258; Zeller, *Der Brief an Die Römer*, 99–100; Räisänen, *The Torah and Christ*, 99.

30. Fitzmyer for example describes sin as personified "as a master who dominates a slave." Similar comments on the meaning of "under sin" are made by Denney and Matera. See Fitzmyer, *Romans*, 331; Denney, "Epistle to the Romans," 606; Matera, *Romans*, 84.

31. The word ἁμαρτία (sin) is used for the first time in Romans in 3:9, which indicates the challenge of the question as to where Paul has already made a charge regarding sin. But if this question is answered at all by commentators, insufficient detail is supplied. Hendriksen for example simply states that Paul has shown that the Jews are "sinners," "under the sentence of condemnation" in 2:1—3:8, and that Paul has shown the same of gentiles in 1:18–32. Osborne is similar, changing 1:18–32 to 1:18–20. But why does Paul provide all this detail in 1:18—3:8 if the only point is that both Jews and gentiles are sinners? That point can be made quite succinctly indeed. The fact of the matter is, Paul has said much more to explicate this notion of "under sin" in 1:18–32, than many commentators appreciate. See Osborne, *Romans*, 85; Hendriksen, *Romans 1–8*, 121.

32. See Donaldson, *Paul and the Gentiles*, 139; Sanders, *Paul, the Law & the Jewish People*, 124; Räisänen, *Paul and the Law*, 99.

be *both* under sin and having sinned. So one does not need to find in 2:1–29 the whole content of Paul's indictment against Jews. These are better retorts than Keck's, who tries to slip the net of such attacks by claiming that 3:9 *discloses the import* of what has gone before rather than summarizing it.[33] On the contrary, 3:9 should be taken as a summary of what Paul has just said.

My contention is that Paul is harking back from 3:9 to 1:18–32, and that his argument there is primarily that humanity in general, and all individuals, are in a *state* that locks them into sinful behavior. They have sinful mental models including their self-appraisal and approval of what is good or right.

At least two conceptual notions can be identified in 1:18–32, which Paul is saying are true of all individuals. First, every human in their natural state is unable to accurately determine the content of the moral life they ought to live. That this is a problem for every individual is seen in that Paul later tells *every* reader that part of the solution is that they need to "be transformed by the renewing of your mind. Then you will be able to test and approve what God's will is" (12:2). So in Romans as a whole, one problem being addressed is that every person is, in their natural state, unable to test and approve what God's will is. It makes sense in terms of Paul's logic that this deficiency is part of what he is describing in 1:18–32.

Second, every human in their natural state has a heart[34] problem that includes desires which lead to impurity (1:21, 24). That this is a problem for every individual is seen in the later argument that each individual must work at not obeying those evil desires by counting themselves dead to sin in Christ Jesus (6:11–12). Thus it is natural to expect that Paul has aimed to communicate in 1:18–32 that *each individual* has this heart problem with desires which lead to impurity.

Given that Paul has sought to identify these two universal elements of fallen human nature in 1:18–32, it is likely that he has identified both of them in 1:21b. For 1:21b "their thinking became futile and their foolish hearts were darkened" mentions both futility of thinking and folly of heart, the second of which likely includes flawed desires.[35] Also, 1:22–31 is an historical depiction of how God justly handed over humanity to these two elements of futility of thinking and impure desires—impure desires in

---

33. Keck, *Romans*, 95.

34. Thiselton reviews sources for the case that the notion of the heart here is much broader and deeper than in modern usage, more than merely emotional or merely intellectual. See Thiselton, *Discovering Romans*, 84.

35. Jewett draws on Liddell and Scott to point out that "heart" appears in Greek texts as the center of "feeling and passion." See Byrne, *Romans*, 74; Jewett, *Romans*, 167; Liddell and Scott, *Greek-English Lexicon*, 877. For more on this verse, see below.

1:24, 26 and debased thinking in 1:28. So taking 1:21b to express these two elements, one can observe a very neat structure where 1:21b sets the agenda for the historical narrative that follows.

This will be developed further below. The point in this excursus has been to address the question, "Without excuse *for what*?" The answer is that all individuals are without excuse for their fallen thinking and their fallen desires, which are two key elements of what it is to be "under sin."[36]

> 21–32 For although they knew God . . .

Paul goes on in 1:21 and 1:22–32 to explain how people are without excuse by means of historical narrative depicting the decline of humanity. While it is possible that 1:21–32 depicts a singular historical narrative, it is more likely that 1:21 depicts the narrative in shorthand, in such a way that it is applicable to every individual, while 1:22–32 expands on the narrative, in such fashion that not every detail is applicable to every person.[37] The notion that 1:21–32 is historical narrative is rare in the scholarship, and so needs defending at some length.[38]

## EXCURSUS: ARGUMENT THAT 1:21–32 IS HISTORICAL NARRATIVE

This claim can be defended in at least four ways. First, the logical διότι, "for," of 1:21 indicates a link between the narrative of 1:21–32 and the phrase of 1:20 "since the creation of the world." Romans 1:21–32 is narrative explaining how events *since the creation of the world* logically support the conclusion (stated in 1:20) that humanity is without excuse. That is, the logical "for" of 1:21 shows that 1:21–32 is historical narrative depicting events "since the creation of the world."

Second, in 1:21 and 1:22–28 the descriptions move forward using a typical narrative verbal structure, the repeated aorist indicative. Campbell writes concerning the use of the aorist indicative in narratives, "While it is

---

36. Note that Paul is not declaring in this passage that people are without excuse for rejecting the gospel, contra Craig. See Craig, *Reasonable Faith*, 50.

37. Two reasons for supporting this dual narrative view are: (1) The asyndeton at the start of verse 22 lends weight to a split at that point; (2) 1:21 works well as a history of humanity concluding with every person's state under sin, while 1:22–32 works well as a general overview of the decline of humanity with examples emphasizing egregious *elements* of humanity's state. So the content of what is actually said supports this split.

38. Frame, for example, describes 1:21–32 as a "history of suppressing the truth." See Frame, *Apologetics to the Glory of God*, 8. My suggestion that 1:21 and 1:22–32 are two distinct narratives depicting the same event, is, however, new.

used in discourse and even in offline information, its main function in narrative is to provide the mainline of narrative proper, outlining the skeletal structure of the story."[39] Aorist indicatives which progress the narrative in 1:21 include "they neither *glorified* him as God, nor *gave thanks* to him, but their thinking *became futile* and their foolish hearts *were darkened.*" In 1:22–28, such aorists include "they *became fools* and *exchanged* the glory of the immortal God for images," "Therefore God *gave them over,*" "They *exchanged* the truth about God for a lie, and *worshiped* and *served* created things," "Because of this, God *gave them over* to shameful lusts," "Even their women *exchanged* natural sexual relations," "men . . . *were inflamed* with lust for one another," "God *gave them over* to a depraved mind." The use of these aorist indicatives fits Campbell's description of the use of aorist indicatives in narratives, since these verbs provide an outline of the narrative.

Third, the tenses here are very likely to depict time, because the aorist tense usually does depict time. While time is not part of the semantics of Greek tense-forms, it is often pragmatically communicated by tense-forms.[40] The context also supports this, which can be seen partly in that the major translations universally render these aorists (in 1:21–28) in past time.[41]

Fourth, the delay until 1:32 of the change back to the present tense not only strengthens the case that Paul is outlining an historical narrative throughout 1:22–32, by working from past time through to present time, it also presents a prima facie case that the history ends in the present day, at 1:32. This conclusion is made more likely still, in that Paul draws his conclusion about the reader (in 2:1) immediately upon reaching the present tense conclusion of his history (in 1:32). As soon as the discussion reaches the point in humanity's history which includes the reader (1:32), a conclusion is drawn about the reader (2:1).

---

39. Campbell, *Basics of Verbal Aspect*, 84.

40. Campbell speaks about remoteness as a semantic value of the aorist tense and points out that "the semantic value of remoteness will be pragmatically expressed as past temporal reference approximately eighty-five percent of the time." Campbell, *Basics of Verbal Aspect*, 37.

41. Johnson writes regarding 1:21, "The tenses of the verbs in this verse, all aorists referring to the past in contrast to the preponderance of presents up to this point in the paragraph, suggest that the apostle is writing of historical events and interpreting the story of man after the Fall. The result is that the words provide the reader with an interesting insight into the biblical interpretation of the spiritual history of man." Unfortunately, Johnson only speaks of this historical regression of humanity in 1:21–23, rather than taking it all the way to the end of the chapter. Johnson, "Paul and Knowledge," 72.

> 21–32 For although they knew God, they neither glorified him as God nor gave thanks to him, but their thinking became futile and their foolish hearts were darkened . . .

The beginning of humanity's historical decline occurred in the time of Adam and Eve. They were created with a sinless knowledge of God, so that they "knew God," and had sufficient knowledge to conduct themselves without sin in God's sight. They are in view when Paul says in 1:21a, "although they knew God."[42] They knew him by direct apprehension, from the world in which they had been placed. They knew him relationally and fully. His revelation was received by them reliably and fully. They represent the historical example of the fact that humans were originally designed to know God, deriving their knowledge from God's reliable revelation of himself and of the moral order in the way the world has been made. Because 1:21a is about Adam and Eve, and not about every person ever to live, it is not necessary or correct to conclude from 1:21a that "God is known by all."[43] Under this reading then one does not need to follow the vast swathe of Reformed scholars who have claimed that every person knows God in some sense. For I have shown the plausibility of the notion that Paul's logic does not flow from *everyone knowing God* to *everyone being without excuse*, but rather from *some knowing God* to *everyone being without excuse*.

With the end of 1:21, the brief one-verse narrative of humanity's history has come to an end. This narrative concluded with two key characteristics of all humanity's state under sin. In 1:22–32, Paul begins a second narrative of humanity, using the first narrative as the outline for the second.

This second narrative begins structurally with a lack of any conjunction linking it to what has gone before. It begins in content by harking back to Adam and Eve's sin—"they claimed to be wise." It is referring to the event when Adam and Eve ate the fruit that was "desirable for gaining wisdom" (Gen 3:6). Through that sin humanity became fools.

---

42. Note that it is common for commentators to see reference to Adam in the section 1:21–32, but not as common to see the section as depicting a history. See, for example, Hooker, "Adam in Romans i," 300–301. See also Dunn, *Romans 1–8*, 72.

43. Contra Frame, *Knowledge of God*, 18. Maintaining that all people "know God" has led to numerous failed attempts to explain how unbelievers both know God and do not know him. For a list of these, see Frame, *Knowledge of God*, 50–58. See also Halsey, *For a Time Such as This*, 63; Van Til, *Introduction to Systematic Theology*, 26; Sproul et al., *Classical Apologetics*, 49–53. In the New Testament field, Cranfield writes regarding 1:21, "Knowing God in the sense that in their awareness of the created world it is of Him that all along, though unwittingly, they have been—objectively—aware." But this concept of unwitting awareness seems at first blush incoherent, and even if it is not, it does not seem fair to condemn someone on the basis of knowledge they never held in a conscious, "witting" fashion. See Cranfield, *Romans*, 117.

In 1:22–31, the people in view are humanity, with claims not true of all people, but true of a *substantial portion* of humanity, as they fell further into sin. For it is clear from the examples of 1:22–31 that Paul does not have in mind all humanity without exception. For example, it is not true that each human has taken up worship of carved idols (1:23), nor has every woman exchanged natural sexual relations for unnatural ones (1:26). It is not even true that the "average" woman has exchanged natural sexual relations for unnatural ones (1:26).[44] The statements of 1:22–31 are therefore best seen as activities which a *substantial portion* of humanity has performed. The examples of wickedness given in 1:22–31 should be seen as *new lows* to which a substantial portion of humanity *progressively*[45] sank, bringing further wrath from God on humanity as a whole.

In the middle of this second narrative, Paul describes the historical revelation of God's wrath[46] by repeatedly using the phrase παρέδωκεν αὐτοὺς, "he gave them over" (1:24, 26, 28). When humanity, historically, has failed to glorify God and has turned to other gods, God in turn has handed humanity over to further captivity under sin. In the first two cases (1:24, 26), God handed humanity over to impure desires and their outworking, with the lusts of 1:26 stronger and more out of control than the impure desires of 1:24.[47] These two cases are depicting how God gave elements of humanity over to particularly darkened foolish hearts (cf. 1:21b). In the third case,

---

44. While 1:22–31 describes lows to which a substantial portion of humanity sank, and is not true of the average person, 1:32 is a statement that is true of the average person. The present tense of 1:32 brings us to present time, so that we no longer have the ingressive character of the aorists of 1:22–31. The ingressive aorists describe things that began to happen within humanity, and as such were not done by the majority, whereas the present tense of 1:32 captures humanity generally, and as such does capture the character of typical humanity.

45. The ingressive nature of some of the aorist tenses in Romans 1:21–31 is picked up in the translations. For example, the NIV and ESV both translate ἐματαιώθησαν as "*became* futile" in 1:21. Many other aorists in 1:21–28 could be translated similarly, for example, "*began* to exchange the truth of God for a lie ..." (1:25), "*began* to be inflamed with lust for one another ..." (1:27). It is possible, but not essential to translate this way, since the progressive nature of the whole historical representation of 1:21–31 is depicted sufficiently by an explicitly ingressive translation of 1:21. For a discussion of the ingressive aorist, see Wallace, *Greek Grammar*, 558–59.

46. Cranfield, following Barth, understands the revelation of God's wrath to occur when the gospel is preached. See Cranfield, *Romans*, 109–10. But Kruse persuasively responds, "The revelation of God's righteousness in 1:17 is more than the provision of information; it mediates God's power for salvation. If we recognize the parallelism existing between the revelations of 1:17 and 1:18, the revelation of God's wrath will involve more than information; it will have concrete expression in history and at the close of the age." See Moo, *Romans*, 100; Kruse, *Romans*, 87–88.

47. See Jewett's notes on these two terms in Jewett, *Romans*, 168, 172.

God handed humanity over to a depraved mind. This depicts how God gave elements of humanity over to particularly futile thinking (cf. 1:21b).

In each case (1:24, 26, 28), Paul depicts this history of the revelation of God's wrath in such a way as to make clear that before God gave humanity over to the different aspects of their slavery under sin, humanity *first* failed grievously. In 1:22–23, it was humanity who failed to glorify God or give thanks to him, choosing to exchange the glory of the immortal God for images. *That* was the reason (διό, 1:24) that God gave them over to sexual impurity. And then it was humanity's accepting of lies, and serving the creature not the creator, which provided the reason (διὰ τοῦτο, 1:26) that God gave humanity over to shameful lusts, including same-sex lusts. Thus the wayward desires which humanity possesses *are humanity's own fault*, historically speaking.[48]

Thus in 1:22–27, Paul has developed another one of the strands of argument which support the claim in 1:20 that humanity is without excuse: because God's active, historical role in giving humanity over to wayward desires was just, there is no ground for an excuse that God has unjustly given humanity these wayward desires.

Similarly, Paul depicts humanity's history so as to make it clear that humanity is to blame for their depraved mind. In 1:28, καθώς should be taken as a conjunction expressing cause: *Since*[49] they did not think it worthwhile to retain the knowledge of God, he gave them over to a depraved mind. It is humanity's own fault that they were given this depraved mind, because they had *first* decided they did not want to retain a godly mind. Various outworkings of humanity's depraved mind are expressed in 1:28–32. These outworkings are concretely expressed, such that they can be expressed in moral commandments like "do not slander, do not hate God, do not murder," and so on. But humanity's depraved mind and failure to obey these commandments is humanity's fault, not God's.

Because God's active historical role in giving humanity over to their depraved mind was just, there is no ground for an excuse that God has unjustly placed humanity in that setting. Note that this is consistent with proposition (iii) at the start of the chapter: problems in humanity's disposition, which hinder the reception of legal revelation, are humanity's fault,

---

48. It is important to notice that this line of logic only applies to humanity considered corporately and historically. It cannot be applied to individuals, for example to claim that it is necessarily an individual's fault when they experience same-sex attraction.

49. The NIV has "just as," while the NIV (1984) and the English Standard Version (ESV) has "since." The point is that humanity deserved to be given the depraved mind because they did not think it worthwhile to retain the knowledge of God.

for Adam and Eve could wholly receive it pre-fall. Our endemic inability to receive legal revelation reliably, is God's just judgment on us for Adam's sin, for our other forebears' sin, and for our individual sin.

The end of the second narrative comes in 1:32, with the introduction of the present tense.

> [32] Although they know God's righteous decree that those who do such things deserve death, they not only continue to do these very things but approve of those who practice them

Ἐπιγνόντες, "though knowing," is an aorist participle, so that the present tense of the New International Version derives from the present tense of the main verb, συνευδοκοῦσιν, "they approve." The Greek present tense does depict present time here, so that one should understand Paul to be speaking of something that humanity, as a generalized whole, knows *today*. The concessive nature of the participle ἐπιγνόντες, "*although* they know," underscores the self-deception of humanity in casting their approval on those they know to deserve death.[50] Even as this narrative describes the progressive new lows to which humanity has sunk, at the end, in the present day, it remains the case that humanity in general still knows this truth: they know that those who act wickedly deserve death.

Paul is not saying that humanity knows that it is God who has decreed this fact. The clarification that it is *God's* righteous decree serves to underscore the true source of the decree, rather than to indicate that humanity in general knows that God is the source of the decree. The assertion of active knowledge, limited though it is, is still profound, and can be stated as follows: there are many throughout humanity who have come to know the truth that there is no person who deserves to live forever.[51]

---

50. Paul is not suggesting that approval of an evil deed is worse than the deed itself, an understanding Jewett, Cranfield, and Middendorf embrace. Barrett tries to avoid this by understanding Paul to mean "I am not speaking only of those who do these things, but also of those who approve." This incorrectly moves the phrase οὐ μόνον, "not only," away from its natural referent, αὐτὰ ποιοῦσιν, "they do these things." Rather, Paul uses the construction οὐ μόνον . . . ἀλλὰ, "not only . . . but," to highlight two different ways in which humanity is self-deceived and contradictory, the second more strikingly contradictory than the first: In the first place, it is not consistent to know that doers of these things deserve death, yet also to do them. But it is even more inconsistent to know that doers of these things deserve death, and at the same time to approve of those people! See Jewett, *Romans*, 191; Barrett, *Romans*, 40; Middendorf, *Romans 1–8*, 143; Cranfield, *Romans*, 135.

51. Note the difference in understanding from those who see a reference here to the death penalty in Jewish and Greco-Roman law (Zahn): Paul is not advocating or referring to such laws. Note also the difference from those who see a threat of death at the last judgment (Daxer, Schrenk, Michel): the point is not directly about the final

A would-be excuse-maker, on Judgment Day, will not be able to say, "*I knew that some of my actions were wicked, but my excuse is that I didn't know what the punishment for wickedness would be. If I'd known it was so serious, I would have tried harder.*" The response can come that you ought to have known that wickedness deserves death, since many came to know that from creation alone. Notice again that this is a reading that underscores all people's just judgment before God, yet does not ground that conclusion in that oft-asserted claim that "all people know God."

While humanity knows that people who act wickedly deserve death, their practice is to continue to do wicked things. But more than that, humanity in general approves of people who do evil deeds. Paul is not saying that humanity in general approves of the individual deeds or character traits referred to in 1:29–31, nor that humanity has lost the distinction between good and evil. My reading of Paul here differs from Calvin, who comments on this verse saying,

> Men had completely abandoned themselves to unrestrained licence in their sinning, and by erasing all distinction between good and evil, approved both in themselves and in others those things which they knew to be displeasing to God.[52]

The flaw in Calvin's explanation is clear when one looks at the world and sees that the typical unbeliever does admit a distinction between good and evil. It is also clear from the passage in that what is approved is τοῖς πράσσουσιν, "the ones who practice," not the practices themselves.

On the contrary, humanity as a whole knows that there is a category of "such things"—evil things like disobeying one's parents, slandering, murdering, and so on. The point is that humanity overlooks such evil deeds and approves of the people who do them, despite knowing that the deeds are evil and that the people who do them deserve death. What humanity does is reject God's disapproval of evildoers *as people*. They do more than refuse to condemn them, they cast a judgment of *approval* on the people despite their wicked deeds.

> 2:1 You, therefore, have no excuse, you who pass judgment on someone else,

---

judgment, but it is to underline the contradiction between approving of people on the one hand and knowing that they deserve death on the other. See Zahn, *Der Brief Des Paulus an Die Römer*, 104; Daxer, *Römer 1.18—2.10*, 62–63; Schrenk, "Δικαίωμα," 221; Michel, *Der Brief an Die Römer*, 108.

52. See Calvin, *Epistles of Paul*, 38.

In 2:1-16, Paul turns to the fact that those who judge others have no soteriological advantage over others. He transitions into this section by underlining that while the reader who judges others might be different from much of humanity, and partially correct in their difference, since they are correct that God does not approve of evildoers, they still have no excuse for their misdeeds, and their state under sin. This is primarily because, like all of humanity, they do evil deeds, and also because they have no excuse for their state under sin. The transition from 1:32 to 2:1 has given commentators much "grief," but the grief can be relieved through understanding the structure and argument of 1:18—3:9.

## THE ARGUMENT OF ROMANS 1:18—3:9

I propose the following outline of the structure and argument of Romans 1:18—3:9:

1:18-32: Humanity has no excuse for being under sin, and no excuse for their evil deeds.

2:1-16: You who judge, though you are different from much of humanity in that you disapprove of those who do evil deeds, are still without excuse since *you* do evil deeds.

2:17-3:8: You who are Jewish, though you are different from much of humanity in that you possess the law and circumcision, are still without excuse since you disobey the law.

3:9: Thus Jews and Gentiles alike are under sin.

## The Transition from 1:32 to 2:1

The primary backward referent of διό, "therefore," is to the fact that humanity practices evil deeds, mentioned in 1:32. The reasoning is as follows: Since you are part of humanity, and thus do evil deeds, you have no excuse before God, even if you are someone who judges others, unlike most of humanity.[53] The reason you have no excuse, is of course, that you do evil deeds.

So the logical connection between 1:18-32 and 2:1 is found in continuity of the subject in view, namely that the reader who judges (the subject of 2:1) is also a member of humanity (the subject of 1:18-32). This continuity undergirds Paul's use of διό, "therefore," in connecting 1:21-32 with 2:1.

---

53. That is, as 1:32 implies, most of humanity are unwilling to conclude from the universal nature of human sinful behavior that all people should be "disapproved of."

Identifying the diatribe style introduced in chapter 2, described for example by Stowers, aids in understanding the rhetoric, but is not sufficient to explain the logical force of the transition from 1:32, since the diatribe style does not require the logical connector διὸ, "therefore," at 2:1. The linguistic repetition of πράσσω, ποιέω, κρίν- and δικαί- words identified by Bassler as marking the continuity of the argument between the first and second chapter is instructive, but insufficient to identify the precise logical connection communicated by διὸ in 2:1.[54]

There is also a discontinuity in subject between 1:18–32 and 2:1, namely that Paul is now addressing in turn two distinct sub-groups of humanity, "you who pass judgment" (in 2:1–16), and "you, if you call yourself a Jew" (in 2:17–29). The reason Paul turns to "you who pass judgment" in 2:1 is that he wants to argue that although such people are in an important respect different from humanity considered as a block, in that they judge evildoers rather than approve of them, yet they are still without excuse and "under sin" (3:9). Likewise in 2:17–29, Paul argues that although the Jews are in important respects different from humanity considered as a block, they too are without excuse and under sin.[55]

> for at whatever point you judge another, you are condemning yourself,

If "you," the reader, are someone who κρίνεις τὸν ἕτερον, "judges another," you κατακρίνεις, "condemn," both them and yourself (2:1). To judge and condemn someone in this context is to do more than acknowledge (the truth) that those who do such things deserve death (1:32). It is also that you κατακρίνεις, "condemn," them; you "pronounce a sentence after determination of guilt."[56]

An important implication can be extracted here by considering the use of τὰ τοιαῦτα, "these things," and τὰ . . . αὐτά, "such things," in 1:32—2:1. The phrases "these things" and "such things" demonstrate that there is, in a certain sense, only one category of wicked deeds. There is only one category of deeds to consider in answering the questions of whether a person deserves death (1:32) and whether someone should be condemned (2:1).

---

54. See Stowers, *The Diatribe*, 86–112; Bassler, *Divine Impartiality*, 131–33.

55. Note Windsor's persuasive argument that 2:17–29 is a single unit, as opposed to two distinct arguments, 2:17–24 and 2:25–29, based on the features that cut across the two-part division. Those features are the term "law," the notion of being a transgressor, and the conclusion of 1:28–29 providing an answer *both* to the question concerning the term "Jew" in 2:17 and *also* to the issue of circumcision in 2:25–27. See Windsor, "Paul and the Vocation of Israel," 144.

56. Bauer et al., "Κατακρίνω," 519.

TESTING PROPOSITIONS AGAINST THE TEXT OF ROMANS 1 AND 2    41

The category could be labeled "wicked deeds," "evil things," "sinful deeds," or the like. As mentioned above, 1:32 demonstrates that humanity in general knows that there is only one such category and knows that anyone who performs deeds within that category deserves death. Additionally, and more clearly still, 2:1 shows that for Paul, condemning a person who does one "kind" of wicked deed implies, according to consistent judgment, condemning a person who does any other "kind" of wicked deed, since in fact there is just one category of "wicked deeds" relevant to condemnation. Thus again, one can see general revelation necessarily overlapping with natural law. For the truths of general revelation imply a need for ethical response. But failure in that ethical response must be of the same "kind" as any other ethical failure within natural law, since there is only one "kind" of wicked deed, the "kind" that deserves death.

> because you who pass judgment do the same things.

This final point is necessary to complete the chain of logic[57] condemning the reader who judges as being without excuse. The point must be added that the reader does wicked things.

Skipping now to Romans 2:14–15, Paul is completing his comments addressed to those who "pass judgment," showing that they too are under sin, since works-righteousness is not a matter of hearing the law, but of obeying it (2:13). Romans 2:14–15 comprise a reasonably self-contained unit.

> 2:14 (Indeed, when Gentiles, who do not have the law, do by nature things required by the law, they are a law for themselves, even though they do not have the law.

To say that Gentiles do not have the law means that they are not guided by the written law of Moses. Yet they do things required by that law, that is, they act in ways showing that elements of the law of Moses constrain them.[58] Paul's statements here are consistent with an understanding that law presses on Gentiles *from without* as well as within. Thus, they receive it at least to some degree, and constrain themselves according to it, although not in a saving way. The dative noun φύσει, "by nature," is consistent with an *internalization* of some of these laws in the thinking, being and character of a person, even though they may not be able to express any of these laws.[59]

57. The logic of all of 1:18—2:1 is in view here.

58. Käsemann is correct in his reading here to say that "it happens repeatedly that those who are without the law do in fact fulfil the intention of the law." Käsemann, *Romans*, 63.

59. This approach agrees with Kruse's observation that in each of the three other

It does not refer to a universal nature of all humans to do the right thing, for such a nature does not exist in people under sin. Yet each person has, in different ways, yielded to certain parts of God's law as it presses on them from creation. The description "by nature" expresses this wherever there is a moral choice made to do right out of a formed nature.

This is further expressed by saying that "they are a law for themselves." The verb εἰσιν, "they are," indicates that the persons themselves are walking manifestations of a law. Individuals do internalize a law over their lifetime, in various ways: It happens through the way God's law addresses them from outside, through the way God has made them as humans to respond to this law, and through the way they conduct themselves over their lifetimes, sometimes receiving, and sometimes resisting God's law. So as they interact with God, other people, and creation, their character is built, dependent on which of God's laws they internalize and respect—and thus "they are a law for themselves."

> 2:15 They show that the requirements of the law are written on their hearts, their consciences also bearing witness, and their thoughts sometimes accusing them and at other times even defending them.)

The plural verb ἐνδείκνυνται, "they show," underscores that God continues to faithfully reveal his ethical truth to this day. It is shown in the Gentiles across the world who in varying ways demonstrate that they subscribe to certain elements of God's law.

The partial internalization of the law of God in the person is expressed in the phrase τὸ ἔργον τοῦ νόμου γραπτὸν ἐν ταῖς καρδίαις αὐτῶν, which can be literally rendered "the work of the law written in their hearts." This is to agree with Witherington when he says,

> Paul assumes that sometimes some Gentiles fulfil some of the requirements of the law, just as Jews do. This does not mean they always do so, or do so perfectly. . . . It does mean that there is some obedience to the will or Law of God among those who are not Christians, with Gentiles in focus here.[60]

But it is not to agree with Schreiner, who takes Paul to mean that *all* of the law of God is written on Gentile hearts.[61]

---

places φύσει is used in the Pauline corpus, the usage denotes "what people or gods *are* by nature." Kruse, *Romans*, 135–36.

60. Witherington and Hyatt, *Romans*, 83.

61. See Schreiner, "Did Paul Believe in Justification by Works?" 147.

To see that it is a *partial* internalization, notice that the argument of 2:14 is "*when* Gentiles . . . do things . . . required by the law, they are a law for themselves." The particle ὅταν, "when," implies that they do not always do things required by the law. Just so, Paul is not asserting that Gentiles are a law for themselves *at every point at which the law of God speaks*. Rather, each Gentile varies in the way he is a law for himself, depending on which elements of the law of God he has internalized. This in turn means that "the work of the law" written in his heart is not referring to the whole law of God,[62] but merely that portion of the law of God which the individual person has bound himself to, so that he seeks to do it. Because this "work of the law" has been internalized *in his heart*, access to it can be gained in "short and easy" fashion.

Each person's conscience—his inner tribunal—has reference to those elements of the law of God which he has internalized, and accuses him, or even defends him, according to his works.[63] This is not to say that conscience is only backward-looking, for conscience can be an inner tribunal regarding hypothetical or potential future acts. But conscience does have a backward-looking aspect to it, and it is this aspect which accuses or defends a person according to his works.

Note that this reading, that the law is to some extent "internalized," is both *allowed* by the passage and *demanded* on theological grounds. For a fully innate view of "the law on the heart" is not tenable. In outline, the reasons are as follows: If all the things of the law were in the human heart innately, apart from and before any interaction with the outside world, external input would not be necessary for human flourishing and development. Yet plainly humans need to, and do, develop their character and moral fiber through interaction with the outside world. A purely innate view of the "law in the heart" leads to an unbiblical emphasis on introspection and mysticism.[64]

---

62. Contra Luther, who takes this section to be about unbelieving gentiles who have the whole law of God written in their hearts, "the knowledge of the law . . . but not grace which enables one to do this." Luther, *Lectures on Romans*, 52.

63. On conscience in the Pauline corpus, see the commentary and footnotes in Kruse, *Romans*, 141.

64. Bavinck persuasively argues that views of a completely innate knowledge of God lead to rationalism or mysticism and have for that reason rightly been rejected by orthodox theologians through history. See Bavinck, *God and Creation*, 68–72.

## SUMMARY

In chapter 1:18–32, Paul is demonstrating that humanity as a whole and individually are without excuse for their evil deeds and their state under sin. He grounds this claim in the fact that God has made his existence and character known plainly, and that humanity's failure to receive this communication has been humanity's own fault. It is an overreach to say that Paul grounds humanity's culpability in a claim that each individual understands God's existence. Paul does not say that. Rather, humanity's fault is described with an historical picture of their progressive descent into ever greater depravity, accompanied by a description of God's proportionate response.

Communication from God about himself was made through creation, that is, from outside of each person, and is universally accessible in an immediate fashion. The matters for which humanity deserves death are not just "theological," but also "ethical," and in the present time, much of humanity knows that those who transgress deserve death.

In Romans chapter 2, Paul addresses those who might consider themselves atypical because of their stance with respect to the law or because of their Jewish identity. In the midst of this discussion, he gives an important sidebar regarding Gentiles who do not have the law of Moses. He says that they nonetheless are a law for themselves. They have internalized *some* of the aspects of the law in the heart, such that they do them and are constrained by them.

## CONCLUSION

Note three key claims of this chapter. The first is the identification of 1:21 and 1:22–32 as two historical narratives, with the second narrative expanding on the first, and both commencing with Adam and Eve, and concluding in the present. This second is to say that it is not necessary to claim that all people "know" or "understand" God in order to say that humanity is without excuse for rejecting him. Paul only claims that Adam and Eve knew God (1:21), and that many, across history, have understood God from what has been made. But that is sufficient to conclude that all should have understood God. If *many across history* could do it, you should have done it too. The third claim from Romans 2:14–15 is to see the "work of the law" "written on the heart" not referring to the *whole law of God*, but only that part of the law of God which each individual has internalized.

I have shown with both the general revelation described in Romans 1:18–2:1 and the natural law of Romans 2:14–15 that they are expressed in ways consistent with the propositions with which I began.

## Proposition 1:

I drew attention to places in Romans 1 and 2 where God's self-revelation, that is general revelation, overlapped with ethical truths, that is natural law.

## Proposition 2:

i. The typical "short and easy" human reception of legal revelation is undergirded by the notion of our being "without excuse" (1:20, 2:1), since if reception of legal revelation were "long and complicated," the time and difficulty to receive it would present viable excuses for not living according to it. Likewise, the understanding that some of the things of the law are written on each human heart (2:14–15) undergirds "short and easy" reception of legal revelation, since that which is written on our heart is easily accessed.

ii. God's universal communication of his legal revelation is buttressed by seeing 1:18–32 as referring to all humanity, and 2:14–15 as referring to all Gentile hearts. Legal revelation's continued dissemination is supported in the temporal phrase ἀπό κτίσεως κόσμου, "since the creation of the world," in 1:20.

iii. The partial, flawed internalization of legal revelation is supported by understanding the aorist, past time of "they knew God" (1:21) as referring to Adam and Eve, but not to all people today. For were the passage referring to all people today, the statement that "all know God" could plausibly be taken as a full internalization of a knowledge of God, rather than a partial, flawed one. But this is contrary to the past time aorist tense that is actually in the passage. Even if this reading of the tense in 1:21 is rejected, however, a partial and flawed internalization by us all suffices to sustain Paul's point, as the whole of this book is seeking to demonstrate. Partial internalization of legal revelation is also supported by reading 2:15 as saying only some of the requirements of the law are written on their hearts, namely, those requirements they do by nature (2:14), which is not all of them. If all of the requirements of the law were written on our hearts, this would not be a partial, flawed internalization of the law, but a complete and accurate one. I have presented a reading where problems in humanity's disposition, which hinder us from receiving general revelation or natural law are humanity's fault, with fault sourced in Adam and Eve, in our other forebears, and in ourselves. In Romans 1:21, it was shown that Adam and Eve could wholly receive the revelation pre-fall. The decline from there was sketched in Romans 1:21–32 as an historical narrative. Humanity's inability to reliably receive legal revelation was depicted as God's ongoing, just punishment on humanity's ongoing sin.

iv. Humanity's culpability for our inability to reliably receive legal revelation is undergirded by reading 1:21–32 as an historical narrative commencing with Adam and Eve and concluding in the present. Such a reading pays close attention to the tenses used in the passage, moving as it does from aorist tense, past time (1:21), to present tense, present time (1:32). This reading sees the passage vindicating God by showing how in various ways humanity through the ages has done things to deserve the judgment which consists in its sinful desires, shameful lusts, depraved mind, and other evil dispositions (1:24, 26, 28–32). This is more plausible than seeing each individual qua individual as entirely responsible for their fallen nature. For some of our evil dispositions clearly derive from the parents and the society that raised us, as well as from the genetics which we inherited from our forebears.

v. The notion that God has manifestly continued to communicate his legal revelation through all of history is underscored in 1:20 by the present passives νοούμενα, "being understood," and καθορᾶται, "have been seen," as well as in the present tense verb ἐνδείκνυνται, "they show," of 2:15. In the latter case, it is the continued existence over time of Gentiles who do the requirements of the law by nature which shows the continued communication by God to Gentiles of his legal revelation.

Thus having traversed all of the propositions with which I opened the chapter, the conclusion is that this reading of Romans 1 and 2 is consistent with these propositions broadly speaking, and is consistent with the proposal to combine the concepts of "general revelation" and "natural law" into a single concept of "legal revelation."

# Chapter 4

# A Theological Anthropology Focused on Perception

In the previous chapter, I stated a set of propositions which are key to this book. To recap, the problem addressed in this book is: if neither general revelation nor natural law are accessible to people reliably, how can God justly judge them for their ignorance and hold them morally culpable for failing to live according to revelation they cannot reliably access?

The first proposition presented in the last chapter was this: that the notions of general revelation and natural law are best treated together as a single unit in posing this problem and answering it.

The second proposition was stated in five parts, the third of which is the departure point for this chapter. That part proposed that people all *internalize* an ethical map approximating "legal revelation" from the reality that is pressing on us, but that we do so with flaws. It is that concept of internalization upon which this chapter will focus. The previous chapter showed that there is exegetical room to accept this proposal regarding internalization, and thus also showed that there is room to move outside of the binary poles that have sometimes been presented. For one of the tensions of pastoral theology has been the perceived choice between saying either that "Paul was wrong" or "Atheists are dishonest in their self-perception."[1] The previ-

---

1. As expressed in the title of the popular work, Comfort, *God Doesn't Believe in Atheists: Proof That The Atheist Doesn't Exist*.

ous chapter made space to move beyond those poles by showing that there is scriptural room to say that atheists are not wrong in their self-perception, but rather they have internalized key aspects of legal revelation inaccurately.

With those planks in place, it is suitable now to introduce the category of anthropology, focused on human perceptions of objects and informed by the language of object relations theory. Commentators and exegetes have not gone here in the past when they have considered the problem addressed in this book. But it is a natural place to go. For the problem of this book is framed in terms of what is accessible to people, that is, what "gets through" in terms of what humans perceive of their world. And this is the focus of object relations theory—a psychological theory of how humans "introject" external objects, so that they become part of ourselves, and "project" aspects of ourselves onto external objects. The introduction of this field will serve two main purposes: First, to show the plausibility of my exposition of the last chapter, especially around the concept of "internalization." Second, to pitch more concretely, albeit speculatively, a proposal for how human perceptions might actually function. The overall proposal of this chapter is that the "projection" and "introjection" of psychoanalysis might be understood as the "internalization" which was described in the exegesis of chapter 3.

## A THEOLOGICAL ANTHROPOLOGY OF PERCEPTION: INTROJECTION AND PROJECTION AS INTERNALIZATION

What follows then is a proposal which sits within the boundaries of exegesis from the last chapter and draws on language from the object relations theory of psychological development. It is in many ways speculative, in that it cannot be demonstrated through exegesis alone. Yet in drawing on categories from analytic psychology, it taps into the evidence base which has been used by those scholars in their crafting of relevant vocabulary and theory.

I begin by asserting the plausibility of the notion, central to object relations theory, that "all people have within them an internal, often unconscious world of relationships that is different . . . to what is going on in their external world of interactions with 'real' and present people."[2] This internal world is plausibly developed through an "introjection" of objects,[3] their behaviors or attributes, so that aspects of the external object are internalized

---

2. Flanagan, "Object Relations Theory," 119.

3. Note that that in the language of this discipline, a person can be called an "object" to distinguish them from the subject who is observing them. It does not imply the "objectification" of people.

as part of the persona. Conversely, "projection" refers to the process of taking aspects of one's internal persona and projecting them onto external objects.[4]

So in a foundational example in object relations theory, a baby's first image of an external object is likely to be her mother, or perhaps her mother's breast. The introjection of the mother is such that aspects of the mother perceived by the child are taken on as part of the child's own identity. The infant believes the mother and the mother's breast are a part of the infant. The infant projects upon the external experience of the breast a false image that the mother and the mother's breast is part of the infant. Growth therefore becomes a challenge, for the child has to realize that their mother is a free agent upon whom they depend. The infant will necessarily develop as they experience further interactions with their mother and the external world. The infant projects not only images upon external objects but also relationships with those objects, such as with the mother, or the breast.

Klein and others speak of the concept of splitting in this regard. Especially in early stages of development, an infant splits both the self and external objects into "good" and "bad," unable at first to cope with a single breast or a mother that is at the same time "good" and "bad." So the infant projects some form of negative relationship with the "bad breast," and a positive one with the "good breast," first introjecting into their internal consciousness, and then projecting upon the experienced "breast," for a time, the existence of two different breasts, and two different mothers. Eventually this dissonance resolves in an image of just one mother with good and bad aspects.[5] But the faulty projection serves for a time so that the child can avoid the unpalatable conclusion that their "good mother" does not respond to their every desire. According to Klein and those who follow her, where this dissonance is not resolved, the result is paranoid schizophrenia.

I embrace the plausibility of this notion that all people form "introjected" images of objects within themselves, from a young age, so that they define themselves in part by what they perceive in objects outside of them. I also embrace the plausibility of the notion that all people "project" images onto external objects. According to this model, our life and psychological health are dominated by objects. Some are real objects, and some are projections of real objects, but all are perceptions of objects. While the language of "projection" and "introjection" is commonly used, the term "internalization" is preferable, if one is referring to real objects. For such introjection and projection would in fact be our processing the character of these real

---

4. Klein, "Schizoid Mechanisms," 101.

5. "Simultaneously, by introjection, a good breast and a bad breast are established inside." Klein, "Some Theoretical Conclusions," 63.

objects and perceiving real objects within ourselves. Moreover the proposal of this chapter is that the "projection" and "introjection" of psychoanalysis might be understood as the "internalization" which was described in the exegesis of chapter 3.

But, according to this model, there are always flaws in the images of objects which we project and flaws in our introjected images of external objects. The images people are developing do not completely and accurately map reality, which is why they are being continually altered and refined. These images develop as the person discovers their world by a series of "experiments." The distortion of reality in our introjections and projections is largely unconscious. It serves the purpose of helping us deal with anxiety, or helping us fulfill our deep desires, or other purposes.

But I now wish to propose that the terminology of introjection and projection might be pushed beyond its usual use in psychoanalysis to encompass introjection and projection of ethical realities. That is, it might be possible to speak of a person projecting upon external objects an image of the subject's own ethical responsibilities. Similarly, it might be possible to speak of a person projecting on external objects an image of those objects' own ethical responsibilities. Lastly, it might be possible to speak of a person changing their self-understanding by introjecting an image of their ethical responsibilities towards God and others. All three of these processes I label "internalization," as depicted in the last chapter.

For example, in this model, given time, a child projects onto their mother not only an image of her as an external object, and feelings about her, but also normative concepts. They see their mother's love and project onto their mother the rightness of her love, as well as introjecting an ethical imperative for them as subject likewise to love others. All of this may be described as "internalization" of ethical realities. The infant sees that their mother communicates commands and disciplines or otherwise reacts when they, the child, complies or fails to comply. From this the child introjects into themselves similar notions of a "command-giver" as well as a "command-obeyer," a "discipliner" as well as "one who is disciplined."[6] The child also projects their own motivations and feelings about these things onto their mother. And in all of this introjection and projection, ethical rights and wrongs are also introjected and projected. These ethical rights and wrongs become part of the identity of the self, not necessarily expressed in words,

---

6. Klein did speak regarding such normative dependence. She wrote, "We keep enshrined in our minds our loved people; we may feel in certain difficult situations that we are guided by them, and may find ourselves wondering how *they* would behave." Klein, "Love, Guilt and Reparation," 338. See also Auestad, "Splitting, Attachment and Instrumental Rationality," 398.

or consciously acknowledged, but there nonetheless. So through experience of the mother's commands and the child's response, and the mother's discipline or lack, and more besides, the child introjects an ethical picture of how they ought to respond to their mother and projects onto their mother how the mother ought to respond to them. The child will test the nature of this ethical picture through experimental disobedience and obedience. And through the mother's responses, as well as through God's communicating ethical truth through the nature of this relationship, the child's internalization of moral reality develops. This will not map exactly to reality, and it will change with experience. But the model in view suggests that there is an ethical reality—an objective ethical reality—which is communicated to the child through God's ordering of the world, such that one can talk of the child's internalized moral representations approximating a reality that is there.

Spero proposes something along these lines when he describes a "Halakhic Metapsychology." The term *Halakhah* is Jewish and can be understood as referring to the ways that a Jew should "walk," that is, how a Jew should live out the Torah. A Halakhic Metapsychology then is "intended to postulate certain working principles which logically precede the study of psychology or psychotherapy as pertains to religious belief and its objects."[7] In describing this metapsychology, Spero writes that "if, from the point of view of Judaism, all aspects of reality are underwritten by a specific halakhic structure, then psychological dimensions of reality must have their appropriate halakhic structures as well."[8] So for Spero, the world has a structure that is "halakhic" in nature, such that the human is designed physiologically and psychologically to receive that which they need to receive to live rightly. Moreover, the world is designed to communicate to the person that which they need communicated in order to live rightly. Here Spero is making a similar claim to my own, using different language. This is important, as it shows that a scholar writing in the field of object relations theory includes the whole range of ethical reality expressed in the Torah as that which might be analyzed through the object relations lens.

It should be understood that it is not adequate to call this internalized ethical map that we all develop an "ethical understanding," since some of what is internalized is unconscious. For example, the *character* and *habits* of the person are intricately interwoven with their internalized ethical map, and these are not adequately described by the term "understanding."

---

7. Spero, *Religious Objects*, 94.
8. Spero, *Religious Objects*, 104.

In the model I am proposing, these introjected and projected images of objects, relationships, and ethical realities are developed apart from the need for any great deal of intelligence. For much of the mapping is developed apart from the need to be able to express it. For most children, it will not be long before many ethical truths are being expressed, and they are expressing elements of their internalized morality to others. However, even the acutely disabled will have substantial internalization of objects, relations, and ethical reality. Thus in this model, there is no correlation between intelligence and ethical superiority. Intelligence enables a person to better articulate their introjected ethical map. It enables them to attempt to map more of the ethical world around them at greater levels of abstraction. It helps them resolve dissonance or contradiction between elements of their introjected map. But whether these resolutions move towards more or less accurate depictions of reality depend not on intelligence, but on other factors such as the person's own character development and decisions, as well as the moral quality of their friends, family, society, and other influences.

In this model, God is an object whose reality presses upon the child from an early age, with some similarities to the objects of the mother and father. Meissner and Rizzuto are scholars who adapt object relations theory to explain how people come to internalize God as an object. They understand introjections of God as an image deriving from internalizations of the parental image. Meissner writes,

> The child has little recourse but to imagine this God in terms of the most formidable human beings he knows—that is, his parents. For this purpose he tends at first to use both father and mother, but increasingly the father as he grows older. . . . There may be direct continuity between the parental image and the God image. . . . Or they may be directly opposed, so that they become antagonistic, usually reflecting underlying processes of defensive splitting. God in this scenario may be utterly good and protecting, while the parents are regarded as mean, ungiving, or unloving. The opposite—idealized parents and devalued God— can take shape as well. Or the good and bad qualities of both God and parents may be seen in various combinations.[9]

Rizzuto expresses it this way based in part on her clinical experience:

> The components of my patients' God representations came from varied sources, and although in most patients one source prevailed, no patient formed his God representation from only one parental imago. Moreover, not only the parent of real life but the

---

9. Meissner, *Psychoanalysis*, 140–41.

wished-for parent and the feared parent of the imagination appear on equal footing as contributors to the image of God. This is because object representations are not entities in the mind; they originate in creative processes involving memory. . . . In Freud's understanding of the subject, and in my own, there is no such thing as a person without a God representation. . . . I postulate that constant dialectic processes between primary object representations and the sense of self bring the . . . child to form some representation of a being "like" the parents (or the mother or the father) who is "above all" and bigger and mightier than anyone else.[10]

Spero presents an object relations model of psychological development—one which explicitly posits and considers the consequences of the truth of God's existence. He writes, "It is . . . conceivable that the divine object becomes known in a developmental manner, mediated *through* parallel interpersonal mechanisms, experiences, and object representations that are in some way preparatory to an encounter with God."[11] For Spero, the discovery that there are beings like yourself comes with the discovery that there is a God-being. That comes to us through our parents, and in other ways. Not only does he expand on Rizzuto's and Meissner's work by considering developmental implications of God's actual existence, he also incorporates "halakhic structures and metaphors"[12] among mechanisms that aid in the person deriving their internalizations of the objective God. By "halakhic structures and metaphors," he means the gatherings of Jewish believers, their interactions, prayers, rituals, scriptural stories, and the like. This enables him rightly to posit a developmental model of belief in God that draws on a fuller range of the kinds of experiences wherein God does objectively communicate himself to a person. Thus, Spero provides viable psychological explanations and examples of how a person might introject an image of God in ways that can be described as *more or less accurate*, because Spero explicitly accepts the reality of God's existence.

With this scholarship in view, it is time to present a number of claims that together represent my "model." These claims sit under the overarching umbrella of "projection and introjection as internalization":

i. Just as a child internalizes images of other objects such as their parents, they also internalize an image of God.

---

10. Rizzuto, *Birth of the Living God*, 44, 47, 50.
11. Spero, *Religious Objects*, 140.
12. Spero, *Religious Objects*, 133.

ii. All of these introjected images imperfectly map the reality, which is why the child keeps altering them as they develop.

iii. In addition to God himself, images of the ethics of how God and others ought to be treated are also internalized.[13]

iv. The accuracy of this ethical mapping has no correlation to the intelligence of the subject.

v. This object and relational mapping can be described as partly intuitional,[14] in the sense that not all of it is expressible or even conscious.

vi. The internalization of God as an object is a phenomenon which draws on experiences in the world such as those with the parent, or the wished-for or imagined parent, or the grandeur of nature.

vii. It is common for people to project elements of the self onto God, crediting God with human desires and traits that he may or may not actually have.

viii. As the child grows, the internalization of "legal revelation" can also draw on various experiences that God himself has designed for that purpose. These include corporate and private prayer, praise of God, and hearing Scripture read, taught, applied, considered, and explained, experience of ritual, such as the scriptural sacraments, and more.

ix. Ethical and theological claims made by a child's family and community are likely to be believed at first by the child, but in time, an adult will revise their conscious and unconscious mappings in accordance with their experience, desires, actions, character, and more.

---

13. Point (iii) is perhaps the most controversial here. See my comments above on Spero to see an example of another scholar making similar proposals, albeit using different language, and a Jewish background.

14. By "intuitional" I mean "formed apart from the processes of discursive reason." This is deliberately less specific than Robert Audi, who is probably the leading exponent of ethical intuitionism. He defines an intuition as a non-inferential, firm, comprehended, pre-theoretical belief. My use of the term here does not require that the "ethical mapping" be conscious, or a "belief" at all. See Audi, *Good in Right*, 35. My wording of Audi's definition is Sinnott-Armstrong's summary of Audi's definition. See Sinnott-Armstrong, "Reflections on Reflection," 19; Audi, *Good in Right*, 33–36.

## POWER TO EXPLAIN OBJECTIVELY FLAWED MAPPING OF LEGAL REVELATION

This model, employing the language and observations of object relations theory, helps in important areas for this work. For it helps to speak of how people might be culpable for our moral failure in areas where God's "legal revelation" has not been internalized by some people.

Concepts and language have now been canvassed to help us say the following: It is plausible, from the standpoint of object relations theory, that all people have the data pressing upon us of God's character, and our ethical responsibilities toward him, yet without all of us having internalized an image of God as truly existing. Plausible reasons for this claim include that God reveals himself through our developing relations with our parents, through relations with our "imagined" parents, as well as through creation in other ways. It is similarly plausible that all people, whether having involved parents or not, have ways in which God's existence presses on them. Furthermore, it is plausible that some but not others will internalize from this data an image of God as truly existing, in accordance with reality, but others will fail to do so. For those who fail to do so, fail in similar ways to those we have seen where people, in a faulty way, internalize object images. Just as in the theorized category of splitting, we plausibly do this partly to aid our ability to act or think in ways we want, partly to avoid the anxiety or fear associated with acknowledging reality, and for other reasons.[15]

This theorized process of splitting, potentially together with other self-protective mechanisms, can help us explain how some people might introject God's self-communication in inaccurate ways. As already discussed, the infant might falsely split and introject two different objects, a "good mother" and a "bad mother," to avoid the guilt and required reparation that should come with some of their attitudes towards their mother. In this case, the child would need to learn to fuse the two images together, accepting the mother as less than reliable but still worthy of love. Just so, an adult might internalize God's self-communication as being that of many weaker and less holy gods so they can avoid having to deal with the fear and requirements of a God who is holy and powerful enough to judge them. Or they might simply suppress his existence for the same reasons.[16]

---

15. In the context of the "split in the image of the mother," Meissner speaks of the "early infantile experience" being "discolored with insecurity, uncertainty, or anxiety," thus laying "the foundation . . . for a basic mistrust that can contaminate and distort the later experience of God." Meissner, *Psychoanalysis*, 140.

16. Meissner writes regarding adolescents, "The degree of superego repression and the intensity of guilt can be reinforced by religious prescriptions and ideals . . .

In similar ways to our responsibilities towards God, one might speak of our responsibilities towards other persons, the world, and ourselves. One might speak of how these ethical responsibilities press upon us, such that all of us internalize images of objects we come across, including maps of how we ought to relate to them. Again, in this model, errors in this mapping will plausibly arise, often unconsciously, partly to aid our ability to act or think in ways we want, partly to avoid anxiety or fear associated with acknowledging reality, and for other reasons.

Thus, it is plausible that all the concepts of "legal revelation" might objectively press upon us in such a way that people all arrive with flawed internal images of that objective reality. The flaws in each person's internalized images will be different, according to this model, yet the commonality of our humanity and the commonality of the "legal revelation" pressing upon us will mean that communities will find substantial but not complete agreement as they try to express the character of this legal revelation.

## POWER TO EXPLAIN CULPABILITY FOR FLAWED ETHICAL MAPPING

It is another step to suggest that this model of internalized "legal revelation" plausibly renders every person culpable when they do not receive it accurately. This is not immediately obvious. For it is initially plausible that sometimes when we internalize reality in a faulty way the blame might not lie within us. For example, the unconscious suppression of memories regarding a traumatic incident in childhood seems not necessarily the child's fault. So it is plausible by parallel that a person's unconscious suppression of "legal revelation" might also be without blame.

It should be clear that the suppression of reality that stems from our *sinful motives* is plausibly our fault. For it is plausible that people will respond to God's self-communication by imaging him in ways that enable them to deny his existence. There are various ways this might stem from sinful motives within us, even if the suppression is unconscious. For example, this suppression might serve an immoral desire not to acknowledge the reality of our guilt, or not to contemplate a punishment our deeds might deserve, or the desire not to yield to God's just demands on us, or some other culpable desire.

Less clear is how a person might be culpable for having inaccurate mapping of legal revelation if this stems from one's anxieties. But there are

---

adolescence is also a time of intensifying religious doubt. Doubt is often an expression of the adolescent's need for autonomy." Meissner, *Psychoanalysis,* 145.

good theological reasons to suggest that self-centeredness, anxiety, and fear in general are part of humanity's fallen character:[17] because of Adam's sin, we all inherit self-centeredness, as well as anxieties which are in fact a distrust of God's goodness towards us, as well as fears of a punishment which we do in fact deserve. I do not have space to consider questions here related to original sin, and in particular how individuals might be culpable for flaws in their character that are sourced in fallen human nature, or from a primal fall of Adam. But it is theologically common enough to take this as a plausible assumption: that we can be culpable for flaws in our nature, even if blame for those flaws rests primarily in others who have gone before us.[18] Isaiah is willing to confess the sin of his own people, as though he is culpable not just for his individual sin, but for his people's.[19] Daniel confesses the sin of his people, committed before he was born.[20] David confesses that he was sinful at birth.[21]

So whether we say that the flaws in a person's ethical map arise from furthering their own selfish desires, or from anxieties and fears, or from some other factor, it is plausible in every case that some blame for those flaws rests in us, as individuals, as well as potentially in other individuals or communities. This is plausibly so even if the flaws in our internalized ethical map come about unconsciously, because the unconscious triggers for errors in this map could still be culpable triggers.

This means it is unnecessary to undergird such culpability by following the long tradition of Reformed and other thinkers who insist that each person is guilty for rejecting God because they know on some level that God is there. On the contrary, from this analysis one does not need to say all humans are guilty because they have something like a computer program with "God and a moral imperative" on their "motherboard." It is enough to say that "God and a moral imperative" press upon us all, and when we do not *receive* this into our "programming," we always bear some blame. In this

---

17. See Phil 4:6, "Do not be anxious about anything"; 1 John 4:18, "Perfect love drives out fear, for fear has to do with punishment."

18. It is not only Augustinian views of original sin that are potential bases for such an understanding. The compatibilism of John Martin Fischer is another system of thought that can undergird such a view. Among his many arguments for the compatibilism of determinism and moral responsibility, he suggests that we can see that moral responsibility requires something different to alternative possibilities because it is not enough that a person has the choice either to help a lady across the street or die. There is a host of literature on this subject that is beyond our scope. See, for example, Fischer, "Frankfurt-Type Examples," 288.

19. Isa 6:5.
20. Dan 9:8–10.
21. Ps 51:5.

way, one avoids the perceived choice between saying either that "Paul was wrong" or "Atheists are wrong in their self-perception." In my model then, God does press the reality of himself upon us, and *some* receive knowledge of him consciously or perhaps subconsciously. But my model does not claim that *all* receive knowledge of him, even at a subconscious level.

The fact that, within this model, intelligence is not correlated with the accuracy of a person's ethical map is also important. For this undergirds the notion that all people are without excuse for their ethical failures. Were it otherwise, a person with low intelligence could plausibly say to God on the Last Day, "But you didn't make me intelligent enough to grasp these moral truths. That is my excuse." And such a defense would have merit. But as things stand, and as depicted in this model, this is not in fact the case. In fact our most deeply held ethical internalizations might come to us through intuitions, apart from conscious reasoning. The plausibility of this notion has been shown by some of the recent research of Jonathan Haidt. Part 1 of Haidt's book *The Righteous Mind* is entitled, "Intuitions Come First, Strategic Reasoning Second." This title reflects the main argument of his book, as Haidt catalogues results of interviews that showed how people, especially in ethical areas, lead with their intuitions and feelings, and then try to justify those intuitions and feelings with reasons.[22] This concept in ethics has important implications: It means that those in less educated countries would not for that reason be less likely to reach sound moral conclusions. Their potentially weaker strategic reasoning would not make them less moral. Also, it plausibly explains why a person could not complain to God on the Last Day that they were born in an age with limited understanding of the world. For example, the excuse will not be valid that "I wasn't born in an era when we understood the science behind the fine-tuning argument for your existence, God. That's my excuse for not following you." The plausible answer will come that God made himself sufficiently clear through what he made, with his character and existence understood apart from complex reasoning, so that the person should have had no need of the fine-tuning argument to believe in God and give him due honor. Just as all sorts of other moral impulses come to us, often truly, apart from discursive reason, through intuition, so does the impulse to worship and honor God.

In a different direction, my model can explain how whole families and communities might for long periods sustain images of ethical reality that are false, while still being culpable for those false images. As a child encounters ethical and theological claims articulated by others in their community, they plausibly create their own beliefs in response. They plausibly

---

22. See Haidt, *Righteous Mind*, 32–60.

begin by internalizing the truth of the claims of their own family and community. However, as time passes, the realities of the truths of "legal revelation" continue to press on them. They plausibly find the claims of their own community more persuasive when they more closely represent "legal revelation." When their own community makes claims against the truths of "legal revelation," the desire to remain in the community plausibly provides internal pressure to maintain an internal dissonance, such that many might do this for their whole lives.[23] However, in time, when presented with true counterclaims about "legal revelation," many will plausibly be unable to maintain the internal dissonance any longer. And so individuals and even whole communities might change their ethical internalizations of reality for the better. Yet when a substantial element of a community has a sinful desire or other motive, often unconscious, to act in a way contrary to the truths of legal revelation, the reverse could plausibly happen. The whole community might internalize new ethical representations of reality contrary to fact. While we are creatures who seek to resolve internal contradictions, there are plausibly some contradictions we will avoid addressing for our whole lifetimes. In all of this, blame for the false ethical images of a whole community can plausibly be traced back to desires, in the community and individuals, to act contrary to ethical reality, in culpable fashion. I have already discussed how Isaiah and Daniel confess not only their own sin but also the sin of their communities. The individual is thus plausibly culpable in the midst of their community leading them into error.

## OTHER WAYS THIS MODEL EXPLAINS REALITY

Turning to other ways in which this model plausibly explains the world, one can consider the mystic tradition, and the polytheistic impulse including worship of idols. This model helps us to understand the preponderance of religions in the world, and why so many in the world seem to have some kind of religious impulse: we can plausibly say that different notions of the divine, in the different religions, resonate with that which people have already introjected and projected in some fashion. For example, in the mystic tradition people seek to grasp God by looking within themselves, shutting out the external world. This plausibly occurs because such people first introject God as an object, then, looking inside themselves, find hints of divine revelation.

---

23. So even cannibalistic tribes managed to remain that way for extended periods. The Indian Hindu practice of suttee was encouraged for long periods, with widows encouraged or forced to be burned on their late husband's funeral pyre.

The model can also be used to explain the preponderance of polytheistic religions: plausibly, it is because we all experience God as a real object that we have aspects of God's revelation internalized within us. So for polytheists, it is plausible that God's demand that we pray to him and honor him has been successfully internalized. Moreover, many have projected onto him that like us, he would want to be honored through offerings of food or physical prostration before him, or representation as a statue. But, plausibly, our anxieties connected with God's judgment or commands lead us to want to limit our perception of his power. Some might achieve this by falsely internalizing a reality of many weaker deities who demand less of us than the true God and invoke less fear.[24]

However, there is great power in the truth that there is one God, especially when that truth is articulated and believed by a community, and connected to the scriptural word. This power has shown at various points in history to be sufficient to overturn widespread community belief in polytheism. Such an explanation for the turn from polytheism to monotheism in the West is more persuasive than that, for instance, of Sigmund Freud. Freud, having discounted the possibility of there being a real God behind our images, throws his lot in with a developmental view of God's image being not even an experience of the individual of their own father in the present but of their forebears' experience of envy. In *Moses and Monotheism*, Freud suggests that Moses was murdered, and that Moses' message and death created a "mnemic image"[25] of an earlier primal father who had been murdered. "When Moses brought the people the idea of a single God, it was not a novelty but signified the revival of an experience in the primaeval ages of the human family which had long vanished from man's conscious memory."[26] Freud's explanation even talks of the "repeat" of "emotions" relating to the "supremacy of the father of the primal horde."[27] Freud is right to recognize that there is something to explain with the growth of monotheism from the time of Moses. But proposing an unconscious transfer of emotion from peoples of an ancient time to the people of Moses' time is speculation lacking evidence. It is more plausible that Moses produced the earliest form of the "written Word of God," which powerfully points to an objective

---

24. We are depicting here a notion of the fragmentation of the God image. Peter Leithart is a theologian who gives one account of such fragmentation. Leithart sees Paul's criticism of paganism and the Torah in Galatians and Colossians as examples of human attempts to partition divine and human worlds and traverse these. See Leithart, *Delivered*, 38–40.

25. Rizzuto's phrase. See Rizzuto, *Birth of the Living God*, 18.
26. Freud, *Moses and Monotheism*, 129.
27. Freud, *Moses and Monotheism*, 133.

reality that was already pressing upon everyone—that there really is a single God who created all and is owed our worship and thanks for all good things.

## CONCLUSION: DRAWING THINGS TOGETHER

Drawing these threads together, numerous gains have been made by considering object relations theory. Recall that the question of the book is this: if neither general revelation nor natural law are accessible to people reliably, how can God justly judge them for their ignorance and judge their moral culpability connected to such ignorance?

Part of this book's proposal is that we *internalize* our ethical map from the "legal revelation" that is pressing on us, but that we do so with flaws—flaws that are culpable, with blame resting either with us or with others who have influenced us.

My consideration of object relations theory has strengthened this proposal in a number of ways. First, the plausibility of there being true communication of ethics, but flawed reception, is strengthened by the insights of object relations theory. For that theory posits objective communication of truth, with human reception developing from our youngest years, but with a filtered reception that is distorted. The parallels bolster the plausibility of my claim.

Second, object relations theory introduces ways of talking about our flawed reception in dynamic rather than static ways, thus enabling us to present a richer picture of our flawed ethical reception: in object relations theory, from the earliest age, we form images of objects, images which we continually refine through repeated "experiments." This is a plausible model to extend into the development of a person's ethical internal imaging. It is a strength that these ways of thinking allow us to consider our development from our childhood, in an account of human culpability.

Third, object relations theory already has categories used to explain how and why we introject and project images of external objects in a faulty way, in particular the category of "splitting." The positing of such a category makes it in turn more plausible that we have similar mechanisms that lead us to internalize, in a faulty way, the "legal revelation" that is pressing upon us.

Fourth, the explanations that object relations theory presents for our faulty internalizations are explanations that can be plausibly linked back to human fault, whether fault in the person themselves or in others who have influenced them in various ways. So selfish desires, or anxieties, or fears of punishment are the kinds of explanations that object relations theorists give for "splitting," yet these can in different ways be traced back to human fault and sin. In saying this, it was necessary to consider human fault and sin, not only on an individual level, but from a corporate point of view, touching on notions of original sin, and being sinful "by nature" from birth. Thus one does not need to say that all humans are guilty because they have the equivalent of a "computer program" with "God and a moral imperative" on their "motherboard." In this way, one avoids the perceived choice between saying either that "Paul was wrong" or "Atheists are wrong in their self-perception."

Fifth, inherent to object relations theory is that we pick things up from an early age by intuition, apart from the workings of discursive reasoning. One strength of this proposal is that such an intuitionist model of ethics makes universal human culpability more plausible. For if our ethics depends at heart on our discursive reasoning ability, then those with lower intelligence are likely to have less accurate ethical maps of reality and an excuse for doing worse in their moral lives. But in utilizing the work of object relations theory, such a conclusion can be avoided. This is supported by Haidt's conclusion that "Intuitions Come First, Strategic Reasoning Second."

So in various ways, this chapter's presentation of "introjection and projection as internalization" has strengthened or given more depth to this key claim: that as people internalize our ethical map from the "legal revelation" that presses on us, we do so with flaws—flaws that are culpable, with blame resting with us as well as with others who have influenced us.

In the next chapter, I will consider more precisely how the claims, thus far, relate to relevant scholarship in the field of philosophical ethics.

# Chapter 5

## Philosophical-Ethical Perspectives

Recall again that the problem being addressed in this book is as follows: if neither general revelation nor natural law are accessible to people reliably, how can God justly judge them for their ignorance and hold them morally culpable for failing to live according to revelation they cannot reliably access?

In chapter 2, I provided a brief and limited history of the concepts of "general revelation" and "natural law." Drawing on Luther, I proposed replacing the distinction between general and special revelation with a distinction between "legal revelation" and "evangelical revelation," and I outlined advantages in this change. This provided terminology fit for the task of simultaneously addressing how both general revelation and natural law relate to human moral culpability.

In chapter 3, I exegeted much of Romans 1 and 2, particularly the passages traditionally styled as the general revelation and natural law sections. I restated the key proposal from chapter 2 as my first major proposition and added a second proposition as a heading supported by five parts. These are central answers to the book's question. The five parts contributed, in various ways, to demonstrating the heading, namely that it is humanity's fault not God's that legal revelation is not accessible reliably. The five parts were (i) each element of legal revelation's content is designed for "short and easy"[1] reception; (ii) each element of legal revelation is communicated universally and continually; (iii) all people internalize an ethical map approximating legal revelation, but we do so with flaws; (iv) problems in humanity's disposition, which hinder the reception of legal revelation, are humanity's fault; (v) God's continued communication of his legal revelation is manifest.

In chapter 4, the focus turned to the third of these five parts, which proposed that all people *internalize* an ethical map approximating legal revelation, a map which is flawed in all of us. That chapter sought to establish the plausibility of this proposal by considering the claims of object relations theory.

To this point there has not been significant interaction with philosophical or ethical ideas pertinent to the issue despite the immediate relevance of such topics to the present discussion. This chapter will seek to redress this omission. Several philosophical-ethical issues will be examined. The distinctions that they afford should provide a level of precision and discrimination through which the present main proposals may be assessed and further refined. It will be demonstrated that in this light the argument being presently constructed may be seen to be even more plausible. The topics from philosophical ethics that will be considered are these: the nature of, and distinction between, "the good" and "the right," the debate between teleology and deontology in analyzing "the right," the human faculties that might receive "legal revelation," natural law, and ethical intuitionism.

## METAETHICS: THE NATURE OF THE "RIGHT" AND THE "GOOD"

The very question this book addresses captures various assumptions in the way it is asked. Notice the wording of the major question: *how can God justly judge them for their ignorance and hold them morally culpable for failing to live according to revelation they cannot reliably access?* There is an inference not only that God can justly judge people's ignorance, but that the ignorance he is judging is an ignorance of right and wrong, and of good and bad. Further, there is an assumption that moral culpability, or blame, springs in part from this sort of moral ignorance. This raises a number of questions that have been treated at length by philosophical ethicists.

A great deal has been written seeking to define "the good" and "the right" and to express the relationship between them. For example, notice the

---

1. Recall from chapter 2 that the phrase "short and easy" was taken from Samuel Hopkins. "Immediate and accessible" is a potential alternative expression.

titles of these two works: The classic work of William Ross, *The Right and the Good*, investigates the meaning of rightness and goodness.² In more recent times, Robert Audi has presented his theory of intrinsic value and ethical intuitionism within a discussion of the relation of the right and the good entitled *The Good in the Right: A Theory of Intuition and Intrinsic Value*.³

It is broadly accepted that one can properly speak of that which is obligatory or commanded, "the right," as well as that which is prohibited or negatively commanded, "the wrong." Transgressions of commands, positive and negative, are the most readily understood moral failures and the most obvious catalyst for God's apportioning of blame.

As well as considering "the right," philosophers have spent much time depicting the way that the doing of the "right" might serve some "good," a "good" that must also be considered in describing the moral sphere. Some philosophers have presented conceptions of "the right" and "the good" which do not sit well with the present argument. For example, there are those who seek to understand ethics by the analysis of the semantics of language alone.⁴ This seems to leave little room for an objective ethics, one that exists independently of human ability to express it. And it seems clear that if God is to rightly judge every human according to a common standard, that standard needs to exist independently of human language ability.

So it is important to state that the conception of right and wrong presently in view is one objectively grounded in God's creation of humanity and our world. God has, in creation, made various kinds, such as birds, land animals, sea, sky, land, light, stars, plants, and humans.⁵ He has made these kinds for various ends, such as to fly, to breed, to serve as habitat or food or markers of time, or to rule over the world in God's image. This ordering of creation into kinds with ends is an important objective grounding of

---

2. Ross, *Right and Good*.

3. Audi, *Good in Right*.

4. Analysis of the semantics of language alone is insufficient to understand the nature of ethics. This is persuasively shown by Adams in an influential article. He used the work of Putnam, who was talking about the meaning and essence of "water": "What is true analytically, by virtue of what every competent user of the word 'water' must know about its meaning, is . . . that if most of the stuff that we (our linguistic community) have been calling water is of a single nature, water is liquid of the same nature as *that* . . . 'right' and 'wrong' are used in something like that way . . . analysis of the concept or understanding with which the word 'wrong' is used is not sufficient to determine what wrongness is." See Adams, "New Divine Command Theory" 137–38; Putnam, "Meaning of 'Meaning,'" 215–71.

5. See Gen 1.

human ethical reality. Humans have always been addressable in common commands because of our common humanity.[6]

Within this framework, the plausibility of the second part of my second proposition should be evident. That part states that each element of legal revelation is communicated *universally*. And indeed, it is *because* every person has commonality of design—*because* they are of a common kind, with a common end—that every element of legal revelation applies to every person. The second part of my second proposition therefore gains plausibility within this biblically sourced conception of the right.

## NECESSARY AND OTHER KINDS OF COMMANDS

Theologians and philosophers have also historically debated God's freedom in giving commands. That is, they have debated whether some of God's commands are necessary, unchangeable by God in all possible worlds, or whether God is completely free to give any kind of command. There is a debate between theological voluntarists,[7] who say that God can decree any kind of moral command he wishes, and their opponents, who say that there are necessary commands that God cannot change, as well as commands God cannot give. This is relevant in the current discussion as follows: If God is free at this moment to change any of his commands, and the creation order is fixed in terms of its kinds and ends, it is difficult to explain how God could let everyone know through creation that his moral will had changed. It seems he cannot, if he has fixed the moral order of creation. It is a very different kind of human who can rightly murder at will, to the kind of human we actually are at present. So it seems God cannot decree it right for us to murder at will without changing the fabric of who we are as humans. For this reason, the present argument is assuming a rejection of theological voluntarism and a fixity of the moral law in line with the fixity of the created order.

So for example, in no possible world could God give the command "hate me and rebel against me."[8] Similarly, "torture that child for the fun of

---

6. Such a position regarding the character of the right is expressed in detail and persuasively by Oliver O'Donovan. For exposition and defense of these concepts, as they apply to ethics, see O'Donovan, *Resurrection and Moral Order*, 35–52. This way of thinking has a long history. For example, Saint Augustine distinguished between the "order of nature" and another way of assessing things "according to the utility each man finds in a thing." Augustine, *City of God*, 334.

7. Ockham argued that God could make it such that hating him was not a wicked act. This seems contrary to passages like Deut 13:1–11. See Ockham, *Commentary*, IV, q. 16.

8. This example of hating God is discussed in Baggett and Walls, *Good God*, 86.

it" is not a command God could give in our world, and presumably not in any possible world. This inability of God derives from his goodness, which constrains him not to create beings who flourish in hating him or in damaging others. This in turn implies that God's character, the kind of goodness he possesses, is a prior conception necessary to properly understand the nature of the right.[9] This set of assumptions helps us see that God can justly judge us for our moral ignorance, if there is a fixed moral law which he is communicating to us all through the fixed structures of his created order. This fixity and the reasons for it underline the plausibility of the fifth part of my second proposition—that God has continued to faithfully communicate his legal revelation.

Yet some commands are not necessary commands.[10] That is, there are possible worlds where God could have given other commands than the ones he has given in our world. There is a possible world where male and female might have been created such that different sexual prohibitions and permissions apply than do in our world, since the angels have a different sexual ethic to humans, and in the resurrection humanity will have a different sexual ethic.[11] Further, within the present world, some of the food laws of the Old Testament could have been different in detail than they are while still serving their purpose, a purpose which includes teaching the holiness of God and the sinfulness of humanity.[12] Thus at least a partial theological voluntarism should be embraced, such that God has genuine choice in determining what is right and wrong for his creation, both before the act of creation and after. This is important to address so it is clear I am not arguing that all the Old Testament ceremonial laws are proclaimed by God through his creation. On the contrary, the Old Testament laws of purity, cleanliness, food laws, etc. do not press upon all people, for they are not stitched into the created order. God gave these commands only to the Jews, and only for a set time, and for a set purpose. The present claim is not that all people should know and obey these laws. Without this qualification, the plausibility of the second part of my second proposition would be diminished. One can only plausibly hold that *each element of legal revelation is communicated universally* if the legal revelation in view is plausibly one which should apply to all people.

---

9. This is to join Adams in rejecting what he calls an "Unmodified Divine Command Theory." See Adams, "Modified Divine Command Theory," 97–98.

10. Contra Craig, who writes, "On the theistic view, God's moral nature is expressed toward us in the form of divine commands that constitute our moral duties. Far from being arbitrary, these commands flow necessarily from his moral nature." See Craig, "Kurtz/Craig Debate," 30.

11. Matt 22:30.

12. See Baggett and Walls, *Good God*, 112.

In the present argument, then, "the right" is best understood at its deepest level as obedience to God's commands—either expressed concretely in the words of his prophets and Scripture or expressed by implication in the created moral order.

## ASSUMPTIONS ABOUT "THE GOOD"

Having discussed questions pertaining to "the right," that is, moral commandments, it is fitting to turn now to matters philosophers have raised concerning "the good." Various notions of the good have been described by ethicists.[13] But the notion of an act having a *level* of moral goodness is the focus here. By this is not meant a level where, for example, life-and-death issues might be of higher importance than honesty. Rather, it is meant that there are elements of our moral lives that cannot be captured by commands alone. This means that one needs to speak of a level of goodness in certain acts because they cannot be spoken of as merely obedient or disobedient. This can be seen in the Scriptures, where one finds numerous matters of morality other than those pertaining to commands. For Scripture speaks of permissions, as well as that which is approved or disapproved. For example, marriage is permitted in 1 Cor 7, divorce is permitted but disapproved of in Matt 19:8–12, and heroism[14] is approved in 2 Sam 23:13–17.[15] These categories indicate to us a scale of actions from "morally better" to "morally lesser," a scale that applies to decisions where there are multiple permissible options.

The example of generosity is a good one to illustrate this. God's law might not require me to give up my coffee money for the month and give the money to the poor, yet I can decide to do it. This is an act that cannot be fully analyzed under the headings of moral obedience and disobedience. It needs to be described as exhibiting a high *level* of generosity. Other approaches might be less or more generous, without being disobedient. So one can speak of "better" generosity, and "lesser generosity." This must be

---

13. Teleological approaches to ethics have rightly been derived from the conception of God as the greatest good. Also important are notions of the good as dynamic flourishing, and the good as a static "way it was meant to be." See O'Donovan, *Resurrection and Moral Order*, 138.

14. This language of heroism was brought into the discussion of supererogation by the seminal article, Urmson,"Saints and Heroes." This article brought the discussion of supererogatory acts back to active discussion in the academy, having been long silent since the heated debates between Roman Catholic and Protestant camps, particularly focused on the practice of indulgences.

15. These examples come from Frame, "Levels," 1–3.

treated under notions of "the good" of generosity, for the command "be generous" is insufficient by itself to canvas the matter.

The freedom that exists within this scale is such that choosing the "lesser" option may not in itself leave the agent bearing "blame" in God's sight, or searching for an "excuse." For in choosing such a "lesser" option there is no transgression. This discussion adds plausibility to the overall argument by embracing an appropriate breadth of the moral sphere in which we live.

## THE FACULTIES RECEIVING LEGAL REVELATION

An important consideration regarding our moral culpability is the level of success with which legal revelation is received by humans. Clearly if no one across the planet ever had any success receiving any aspect of general revelation, claims for human culpability would be undermined. But it is reasonably well-accepted that we have a mixture of failure and success in receiving the content of general revelation. So, one can then ask this question: how unsullied do our various faculties need to be for us to be rendered culpable for our immoralities? One should speak similarly to Hermann Bavinck: humanity has not "become devils who, incapable of being re-created can never again display the features of the image of God. Instead . . . they remained essentially and substantially the same, that is, human, and kept all their human components, capacities, and powers, the form, character and nature, the set and direction of all these capacities and powers."[16]

Without the existence of human faculties, or as Bavinck calls them, "components, capacities and powers," that are designed to enable the various aspects of our moral functioning to occur, it seems a person could not be held accountable. For a viable universal moral culpability, faculties like the will, conscience, self-consciousness, rationality, emotion, language comprehension, and moral "vision" must exist in every person, even if those faculties are damaged in some way through sin or otherwise.

But what can one say about which faculties are addressed by legal revelation? This can be answered by considering what is involved in "seeing" that we should not murder. Such seeing involves the senses, the mind, and the understanding, at least. But our moral responsibility in regard to murder in fact goes beyond these faculties. For it is also true that our will should not *decide* to kill, that we should not *desire* to murder, that we should not *find joy* in hearing of murder, much less in committing it, that we should be *more outraged* at a murder than at lesser sins, and that *our conscience* should tell us which potential acts of ours should be considered murder, or

16. Bavinck, *Sin and Salvation*, 140.

which acts of our past might have led to us killing. So, the proposal being put here is that for every person to be morally culpable before God, God's legal revelation must address all of our faculties—*our whole person*—such that *our whole person* is exposed to all the ethical communication needed to live rightly. An alternative might be that our whole person is addressed *via* a particular faculty, such as the will or the rationality. However, while other faculties *can* be addressed via our rationality, as the Scriptures do, *a direct address of the relevant faculties* is the "point of contact" for legal revelation. Consider those faculties which our rationality or will cannot directly address, such as our emotions. It is wrong for me to feel joy at murder. But the right emotion does not come to me primarily by command of my will or by reasoning myself into it. We do not primarily *instruct* ourselves to feel sadness and anger at a murder, nor do we typically reason ourselves into such emotions. They are meant to directly rise up in us. Just so, God's legal revelation must address our emotions directly so that the character of the situation and of the created order presses upon us the need to feel sadness and anger at murder. This is how we are, in the first instance, meant to obey commands like "Mourn with those who mourn."[17] We are meant to be able to obey them because God's legal revelation has addressed our emotions directly, bringing us to mourn at the fitting time. Since every faculty is addressed in this way by legal revelation, a person can be held culpable for sinful responses, no matter the faculty from which they stem.

Pannenberg brings support of a certain kind to this proposal: He critiques the treatments of revelation under the heading of the "Word of God" by speaking of the ways God reveals himself in the Old Testament.[18] He considers the heading the "Word of God" to be too imprecise to capture all that needs to be said. This is because Scripture records multiple modes through which humans experience God's self-revelation. In the Old Testament alone, Pannenberg highlights: (1) intuitive manticism (e.g., dreams and prophetic trances) where God is not seen or heard, (2) such experiences in which God is also seen and heard (e.g., the calling of the prophets), (3) the communicating of the divine name to Moses, (4) the revelation of the will of God (e.g., at Sinai), and (5) the prophetic word of demonstration.[19] It is not necessary to endorse Pannenberg's categories to accept his point that Scripture records multiple modes and faculties through which humans experience God's self-revelation. Pannenberg is aiming in his discussion,

---

17. Romans 12:15.

18. Barth's treatment of the revelation of God is the foil against which Panneberg argues. See Pannenberg, *Systematic Theology*, 1:227; Barth, *Church Dogmatics*, 125–86.

19. Pannenberg, *Systematic Theology*, 206.

especially against Barth, to point out that revelation is more than the speech of God—more than even "the act of God as the speech of God."[20] My related point is that multiple human faculties are addressed by God in Pannenberg's examples of special revelation. And if this is so in his special revelation, it makes sense that it also be so in general revelation and natural law—in the whole of "legal revelation."

The broader point is that it is very plausible that our moral culpability extends beyond simple failure in one of our "leading" faculties, such as our mind or our will, and extends to every faculty. This indeed is my claim. But this means in turn that one should say that God's "legal revelation" is a communication to our emotions, affections, conscience, self-consciousness, will, sense of beauty and all our faculties which pertain to our moral life—to our whole person. "Legal revelation" addresses every human faculty, just as every human faculty has in turn been damaged by sin. This breadth of legal revelation, addressed to our whole person, coordinated with the assumption that sin infects our whole person, gives greater depth and therefore greater plausibility to my claim in part 4 of proposition 2, that humanity is to blame for our flawed mapping of legal revelation.

As an aside, note that the term "legal revelation," while suitable within the present work which gives it context, may cause confusion if used outside it. For the word "legal" can be taken to necessarily involve linguistic acts. Similarly, the term "revelation" can equivocate if it becomes inadvertently conflated with "special" Scriptural revelation, with linguistic content easily assumed. Yet as this discussion of "faculties" should have made clear, the phenomena I am seeking to elucidate may be pre-linguistic, or sub-linguistic for each human individual. To avoid confusion, others may therefore wish to use terms such as "natural accountability" or "created awareness" to denote my concept of "legal revelation."[21]

## NATURAL LAW AGAIN

The major question for this book is posed in terms of natural law, but so far my analysis of the concept has been limited. In his study of the medieval use of the term *ius naturale*, Rupert Kilcullen describes the notion of natural law as "the universal and immutable law to which the laws of human legislators,

---

20. Pannenberg proposes "Revelation as history" to replace "Revelation as the Word of God" as the overarching theme under which the doctrine of revelation should be treated. Pannenberg, *Systematic Theology*, 227–28.

21. These suggestions derive from Andrew Cameron's comments in marking the original thesis from which the present work has been derived.

the customs of particular communities and the actions of individuals ought to conform."[22] This definition brings to attention the importance of the content and immutability of natural law by defining natural law as immutable and by defining its content in terms of the bodies who ought to conform to it. I will expand on these two points in turn. The content of natural law is important to address in the current argument, especially in order to understand the practical implications. Its mutability is important, since if God's legal revelation is subject to great change, it is hard to see how humanity can be to blame for not grasping concepts which might be different today from yesterday or tomorrow.

## The Content of Natural Law

The above definition of natural law, then, should be understood to be filled with concrete content, expressed in the following three subsets: The first subset of natural law is the set of commandments which are incumbent on all people to obey, no matter what their background or culture might be. An example member of this set is the commandment "Do not steal." The assumption is that while different cultures handle the ideas of possessions and stealing differently, nonetheless the command itself "Do not steal" is understood across all cultures and is incumbent on all to obey. Another example member of this set is the command "Honor and give thanks to God." This latter command might have been treated under general revelation, rather than natural law, appearing as it does in Romans 1. However, one of the distinctive elements of the present argument is the notion that these have been artificially separated. As a result, I am explicitly defining natural law in a way synonymous with my own term "legal revelation," encompassing *all* the commands of the moral law.

The second subset of natural law is the set of virtues and vices, understood not as commandments to be virtuous or to avoid vice, but as subsets of "the good" or "the bad." So for example although different cultures have different ways of expressing generosity towards others, and although some people are in a better economic position to express generosity than others, yet across all people, the more generous act is, other things being equal, the morally better act. Generosity is an expression of "the good," as well as an expression of "the right" as follows: While there is a commandment "Be generous," there is also a scale of generosity which cannot be defined solely in terms of duty. For oftentimes a person has a choice of acts, some more

---

22. Kilcullen, "Natural Law," 831.

and some less generous, wherein none of those permissible acts are either prohibited or commanded.

Conversely, laziness is an expression of "the bad." For although different cultures have different understandings and expectations of a right level of work that a person ought to do, and the character of that work, yet across all people, the lazier the set of acts, other things being equal, the morally worse the set of acts. While there is a commandment "Do not be lazy," there is also a scale of laziness which cannot be defined solely in terms of duty. For oftentimes a person has a choice of sets of acts, some sets more and some less lazy, wherein none of those acts is individually prohibited or commanded.

The third subset of natural law is the set of all truths that must be understood by a person for them to understand the two subsets of natural law outlined above. For example, a person cannot understand the commandment against stealing without understanding the concept of possessions. This means further that the truth "possessions exist" is an element of natural law—it must be grasped in order to grasp the truth of the commandment "Do not steal." Likewise, a person cannot understand the command "Worship God and give thanks to him" without accepting the truth "God exists." So the truth "God exists" is an element of natural law. This in turn means that the content of natural law is broader than just statements of commands, virtues, and vices, for these must not only be stated but also understood.

Notice that the breadth of content described here is wide, and necessarily so in order to cover the breadth of the ethical life. The breadth includes elements traditionally associated with general revelation rather than natural law, again necessarily so, for both these elements must be considered in a full treatment of the ethical life. This points to the plausibility of proposition 1, that the notions of general revelation and natural law are best treated together as a single unit in posing the problem addressed in this book and answering it.

## The Immutability of Natural Law

The degree of mutability of natural law is also important for present purposes. This is because a great variability in natural law would seem to make it less plausible that each person ought to live according to a law that varies so much. The degree of mutability of natural law was disputed in medieval and Reformation theology. Pointing to the change of circumstances, before and after Adam's sin, Alexander of Hales proposed that at least some elements of the natural law prescribed different precepts in different circumstances.[23] Bonaventure[24] and Duns Scotus[25] took a similar position.

Aquinas[26] and Calvin took the opposite side, arguing for the immutability of natural law and the Decalogue. Calvin wrote,

> We must bear in mind that common division of the whole law of God published by Moses into moral, ceremonial, and judicial laws.... The moral law (to begin first with it) is contained under two heads, one of which simply commands us to worship God with pure faith and piety; the other, to embrace men with sincere affection. Accordingly, it is the true and eternal rule of righteousness, prescribed for men of all nations and times, who wish to conform their lives to God's will.[27]

While it is easier to understand a fixed natural law from Aquinas's and Calvin's point of view, it is not necessary to take their side of an *entirely immutable law across salvation history* for this term to make sense. It is enough that the content of natural law be fixed after the fall, *for those relying solely on legal revelation*. So Adam and Eve in their state of integrity may have lived under a content of natural law with differences to that which existed after the fall, due to changes in creation with the advent of the curse. Also, there may also be some differences between the requirements of natural law generally communicated to all and the requirements of those living under the New Covenant. These differences are grounded in the changed nature of Christian people who have received the morally enabling Holy Spirit.[28] But these differences do not imply a mutability of the natural law communicated to all through creation.

At least three features point to an essentially unchanged natural law across the ages. First, God is the same across the ages. So there is a constancy in him which undergirds constancy in his law. Aquinas's use of the

---

23. Alexander of Hales et al., *Summa Theologica*, 348–52. Alexander himself followed Gratian and Augustine in this.

24. Bonaventure, *Opera Theologica Selecta*, 2 Sent., dist. 44, a. 2, q. 2, ad. 4, 1051.

25. Scotus drew on Gratian and Augustine in arguing that natural law implied different approaches to property for the state of innocence as compared with the fallen state. See Scotus, *Will and Morality*, 63, 220.

26. For Aquinas, "precepts" of both the natural law and the Decalogue are unchangeable and indispensable, albeit that God can determine which instances of action should rightly be counted as murder, theft, etc. See Aquinas, *Summa Theologica*, I-II, q. 94, a. 5; I-II, q. 100, a. 8.

27. Calvin, *Institutes*, IV.xx.14–15.

28. In view here are commands unique to the New Testament era, such as 1 Corinthians 7:29–31.

notion of "eternal law," as discussed in chapter 2, can for this reason be embraced, broadly speaking, and helps to secure the immutability of God's law. Second, humanity is essentially the same across the ages. Humanity is described as being in the image of God before the fall,[29] after the fall,[30] and after the pouring out of the Spirit.[31] The commonality of humanity undergirds a common natural law applying to that humanity. Third, while the New Testament does at times amend and qualify the Old Testament law of God, there are also confident restatements in the New Testament of Old Testament law, without qualification.[32] This implies that the New Testament assumption is one of continuity of law between the Testaments.

A natural law, unchanged across the ages, does have a plausible biblical basis, then. It is beyond the present scope to consider the question of how the content of natural law relates to the content of Old Testament law, but note that a variety of views on the relationship between biblical law and natural law are consistent with my proposed notion of natural law.

This notion, that a basically immutable natural law plausibly exists, undergirds the plausibility of the second part of my second proposition: that each element of legal revelation is communicated universally and continually. The immutability of the natural law across time owes to God's faithfulness in maintaining it and communicating it. God's faithfulness in this regard is a key ground for human culpability in failing to keep that law, the human culpability which is the overall claim of my second proposition.

## How the Natural Law Is Known—Innateness in Humanity?

Historically, theologians have found the definition of natural law hard to separate from the topic of how we know the natural law. Scotus, for example, explicitly defines natural law in terms of how it is known:

> A practical truth of natural law is either one whose truth can be ascertained from its terms (in which case it is a principle of natural law, even as in theoretical matters a principle is known from its terms) or else one that follows from the knowledge of such truths (in which case it is a demonstrated conclusion in the practical order). And strictly speaking, nothing pertains to the law of nature except a principle or a conclusion demonstrated in this fashion.[33]

29. Gen 1:26.
30. Gen 9:6.
31. Col 3:10.
32. 1 Cor 9:9; cf. Deut 25:4.
33. Scotus, *Will and Morality*, 195.

His last sentence states that it is a necessary condition of any truth pertaining to the law of nature that it be ascertained or demonstrated in a certain way. Such a definition of natural law in terms of how the truths may be known is here rejected. However, the strong links some make between natural law and how that law is known make it important to comment in this area.

The present assumption is that it is not necessarily possible, by reason alone, to demonstrate each element of the natural law to a third party, from shared premises. Similarly, it is not necessarily possible, by reason alone, for a person to demonstrate each element of the natural law to themselves. But this assumption raises a further question: if elements of the natural law are not necessarily knowable by reason alone, but yet, on consideration, ought to be embraced, by what means does God expect us to come to the knowledge of such truths?

As was argued in chapter 3, the participle γνόντες in Romans 1:21, "although they knew," may be taken to refer to knowledge that resided in Adam and Eve rather than to knowledge that resides in every person today. Even if this reading is rejected, it is not necessary to take Paul to intend a perfect internalization of the knowledge of God in us all, in order for his argument to stand. A partial and flawed internalization is sufficient. So there is no impetus from that passage, which is the main scriptural impetus for the view, to conclude that all people "know" God today. One can, however, endorse the term "innate" if it is taken as follows: that humans are designed to be able to know each individual element of the natural law apart from Scripture, being potentially able to affirm any true command, virtue, or vice expressed to them and even discern that element for themselves. This potential ability draws on both the "innate" humanity of the person and their upbringing within their community. This potentiality is however often lost due to people's own fault and sin. Note how this "innateness" question relates to potential excuses for wrongdoing: on the one hand, a "known-deep-down-by-all" concept of innateness seems to secure the notion of no-excuse, since it ensures that whatever we ought to know is already known "within us," meaning we cannot plead ignorance. But on the other hand, such an "innateness" doctrine seems not to fit our experience, if one is to believe those people who insist they have never known some of these truths.

Calvin's view of the innateness[34] of the natural law led him to be too optimistic about human knowledge when he wrote the following:

> Since man is by nature a social animal, he tends through natural instinct to foster and preserve society. Consequently, we observe

---

34. For discussion of how Calvin saw knowledge of the natural law as innate, see Helm, "Calvin and Natural Law."

that there exist in all men's minds universal impressions of a certain civic fair dealing and order. Hence, no man is to be found who does not understand that every sort of human organization must be regulated by laws, and who does not comprehend the principles of those laws. Hence arises that unvarying consent of the nations and of individual mortals with regard to laws. For their seeds have, without teacher or lawgiver, been implanted in all men.[35]

On the contrary, it is evident that men and women can be found who do not understand the need for laws and do not comprehend the principles of those laws. There are genuine examples of anarchists and nihilists, albeit they are rare and they cannot in practice live out the implications of their stated beliefs. John Lennon's famous song "Imagine," for example, seems to indicate his preference for no countries and therefore no laws.[36] The consent Calvin claims to be "unvarying" is not so. Thus a "known-deep-down-by-all" view of innateness is best rejected.

Instead, it is better to accept the exegesis of Romans 1:21 outlined in chapter 2, understanding that the passage merely claims that Adam and Eve "knew God." Through this, or other means, the claim can be avoided that all people "know God." The manner then in which all people are meant to come to knowledge of the natural law is by intuition upon contemplation of the world, themselves, and the particular element of the natural law in question.

For those who follow Calvin's claims of innateness of natural law, there remains the difficult task of contending that people across the world in fact know many truths which they say they do not know. If they press innateness claims to their limit, they will face the additional difficulty that a completely "innate" theology of the knowledge of God tends towards mysticism or rationalism and has for that reason many weighty historical voices militating against it.[37]

## Obligations to God and Humans in the Natural Law

Some may object that the assumptions made so far imply that it is as easy to know our obligations towards God as those towards our fellow humans.

---

35. Calvin, *Institutes*, II.ii.13.

36. The consent Calvin claims to be "unvarying" is not so. Thus a "known-deep-down-by-all" view of innateness is best rejected.

37. Bavinck persuasively argues that views of a completely innate knowledge of God lead to rationalism or mysticism and have been rejected by orthodox theologians through history. See Bavinck, *God and Creation*, 68–72.

Indeed, the assumption-set laid out in this chapter embraces the view that our obligations toward God and fellow humans can be treated in the same way in at least two respects: in regard to the possibility of our knowing them, and in regard to our being culpable for failing to meet them. However, this is not to imply that our obligations to worship and thank God for our blessings are as easy to grasp as our obligations not to steal or injure other people. It is not to disagree with Calvin when he distinguishes "earthly things"[38] from "heavenly things,"[39] and argues that humanity has natural tendencies to rightly comprehend the former in far greater degree than the latter.[40] But it is to say that for each element of the moral law, there have been individuals in history who have come to know that law or that value apart from the written word of God. This is the case for *both* our obligations towards other humans *and also* our obligations towards God.

## ETHICAL INTUITIONISM AND ACCESSIBILITY TO REVELATION

Whichever positions are taken on the content, immutability, and reception of natural law, the easiest way to endorse the proposals of this book is by endorsing a generic ethical intuitionism, a position which has seen a resurgence in recent years.[41] This is especially important for the plausibility of part 1 of proposition 2, that each element of legal revelation's content is designed for "short and easy" reception. For the "short and easy" reception of at least some moral truths is of the essence of what ethical intuitionism claims.

Already discussed above was the importance of the assumption that elements of natural law are in a certain sense knowable,[42] even if they are not demonstrable. But if there are elements that are not demonstrable, it is hard to see how they can be known other than as intuitions. The kind of

---

38. Meaning something in the neighborhood of "our obligations towards fellow humans."

39. Meaning something in the neighborhood of "our obligations towards God."

40. Calvin, *Institutes*, II.ii.13.

41. See for example the various contributions in Stratton-Lake, *Ethical Intuitionism*. See also Huemer, *Intuitionism*.

42. By "knowable" we mean knowable *to some but not to all people*. That distinction is important, because some people have, through their evil behavior, become blinded to particular elements of natural law and so are unable to know them. But this does not mean that the moral truth in question is unknowable in the pertinent sense. For example, a mafia boss, through his life of crime, may well have come to the point where his is unable to discern the truth of the natural law "Do not steal." It is for him, at least while he refuses to repent, a moral duty he cannot know.

intuitionism in view here is one like the generic intuitionism defined by Robert Audi. He writes that an intuition is a non-inferential, firm, comprehended, pre-theoretical moral belief.[43] Note that an intuition is here understood as a *belief*, not as a belief-forming capacity, as in some usage. This pre-theoretical criterion could be helpfully amended to a "non-theoretical" criterion. With his pre-theoretical point, Audi is aiming to secure the notions that "intuitions are neither evidentially dependent on theories nor themselves held as theoretical hypotheses." Both of these notions are secured adequately by using the term "non-theoretical," which has the added benefit that it is easier to grasp than the alternative, pre-theoretical.[44]

Audi defines "intuitionism as an ethical theory to be, in outline and in a minimal version, the view that there is at least one moral principle that is non-inferentially and intuitively knowable."[45] Further he defines "generic intuitionism" as the "stronger view, on which there is a group of at least several such moral principles."[46] Audi's work has been of such note that he leads a movement called the "new intuitionism." He has built on the work of previous champions of intuitionism such as W. D. Ross and increased its plausibility in particular by arguing that the self-evident does not have to be unprovable.[47] This greater plausibility of intuitionism in turn bolsters the plausibility of part 1 of my second proposition, that each element of legal revelation's content is designed for "short and easy" reception. Of course, an ethical intuitionism of a less refined character long predates modern times.[48]

## CONCLUSION

I have traversed a wide range of questions in moral philosophy in this chapter. These included the nature of and distinction between the good and the right, the debate between teleology and deontology in analyzing the right, the faculties that receive legal revelation, the content, mutability, and reception of natural law, and ethical intuitionism.

43. Here we are drawing on Sinnott-Armstrong's neat summary of Audi's quite wordy definition of an intuition. See Sinnott-Armstrong, "Reflections on Reflection," 19; Audi, *Good in Right*, 33–36.

44. See Audi, *Good in Right*, 35.

45. Audi, "Intuitions," 172.

46. Audi, "Intuitions," 172.

47. Audi, "Reason and Experience," 3.

48. As example of such direct intuition, Augustine writes, "the intellectual mind is so formed in its nature as to see those things, which by the disposition of the Creator are subjoined to things intelligible in a natural order, by a sort of incorporeal light of a unique kind." Augustine, *The Trinity*, XII.15.

Sticking closely to the views of Adams and O'Donovan, I proposed that God's commands—"the right" being best understood at its deepest level as obedience to God's commands—are either expressed concretely in the words of his prophets and Scripture or expressed by implication in the created moral order. I proposed a partial theological voluntarism, with some but not all of God's commands regarded as necessary.

I took the position that there are human faculties which must exist in every person, such as the will, conscience, self-consciousness, rationality, emotion, language comprehension, and moral "vision," though these faculties are damaged in various ways. Since the fall, these faculties have kept their form, character, nature, set and direction as "human faculties," though each is sullied by the fall. "Legal revelation" addresses our whole person, addressing every faculty directly with its own instruction set. Human culpability is undergirded by this fact that every faculty is addressed by legal revelation, since there is no excuse that God's communication was unfit for purpose. I indicated that such a depiction of "legal revelation" is such that outside the context of this present work, others may prefer to use alternative terms such as "natural accountability" or "created awareness."

I outlined the content of natural law in a way that includes both the "ethical" and the "theological," in tune with the thrust of this book, painting a broad canvas of the ethical life. I explained how the potential mutability of natural law across the ages of salvation history fails to undermine the plausibility of my argument.

In terms of the justification of ethical positions, I proposed an ethical intuitionism which is defended by Robert Audi in the modern era and Augustine in the classical era. The level of precision and development of the "new intuitionism" under Audi and others provides support to my proposal that legal revelation can be received in "short and easy" fashion. For the essence of an intuition is that it is non-inferentially and intuitively knowable.

As I expressed these positions, I referred specifically to how various positions supported the plausibility of my claims. Thus, I have shown that the major thrusts of this book can be held while answering significant questions in philosophical ethics in plausible ways. This leaves us in a more confident place to conclude that though neither general revelation nor natural law are accessible to people reliably, God can still justly judge them for their ignorance, and judge their moral culpability connected to such ignorance.

With this ground covered, the next chapter will seek to draw out some ramifications of what has been argued.

# Chapter 6

## Applications for Confident Presentation of the Gospel

This chapter will seek to unpack some of the implications of my argument. In particular, I wish to bring out implications that aid Christians in affirming their Christianity with confidence. Two conversation partners will aid us in this task. They are Lesslie Newbigin and Alistair McGrath. They share the strength of having written about how mission and apologetics should look in a modern, pluralist culture.

Newbigin spent time in the mission field in India, a pluralistic setting which helped clarify his thinking, and equipped him in his task to help Western churches keep their missionary confidence in the midst of great cultural transition. His "The Gospel in a Pluralist Society" is his most developed work in setting out his approach and rationale.

McGrath's strengths include his background as a converted former atheist, his deep grasp of the discipline of theology, his astute reading of popular intellectuals, and his ability to write at an accessible level. In a great number of his works, in particular, in his *Mere Apologetics*, McGrath brings these strengths to bear in order to aid Christians in their public defense and presentation of the gospel.

Thus these writers bring good and distinct approaches to the setting forth of the gospel of Jesus. By interacting with them, it will become clear how the theological proposals of the previous chapters yield practical and liveable application and strengthen the case for Christian outreach to all peoples, even in the pluralist settings found in the modern West.

I will assess these two writers, keeping in mind the distinction between legal and evangelical revelation that has been a centerpiece of this work. Recall that in chapter 2, I defined "legal revelation" as "the expressible communication of God to all, communicating that which humanity needs to live a righteous life under the covenant of works." I defined "evangelical revelation" as "the expressible communication of God, communicating that which humanity needs to live a righteous life under the covenant of grace."

## LESSLIE NEWBIGIN

Newbigin lived from 1909 to 1998. He spent much of his working life as a missionary in South India. In this context, he had to wrestle with the practical questions of how to bring Christianity to a culture that possessed a variety of religious expressions. On his return to the United Kingdom, he wrote about how the church in the West should bring the gospel to its post-Christian culture. His writing is influential among modern writers in missional ecclesiology,[1] with his most rounded such work being *The Gospel in a Pluralist Society*. His stated aim in that volume is to "examine the roots of this culture which we share and suggest how as Christians we can more confidently affirm Christianity in this intellectual culture."[2]

## THE GOSPEL IN A PLURALIST SOCIETY

Early in the book, Newbigin restates the case, originally from Alan Bloom, that the most significant sign that relativism and subjectivism reign in the West is that the language of "values" has replaced the language of "right" and "wrong."[3] Bloom traces this change through Max Weber to Nietzsche.[4] In the West, the factual ontological basis for using the language of "right and wrong" has been removed. So all that remains is the will to power, that is, ambitious pursuit of the highest possible position. The present view then is that we cannot use the language of right and wrong any more in the West because it is seen to have no basis in the "facts" as we understand them.

---

1. See, for example, the tone of the citations of Newbigin in Hill, *Salt, Light, and a City*, xi, xvi, xvii, 111, 153, 154, 219, 221, 222, 232, 237, 260, 262.
2. Newbigin, *Gospel in a Pluralist Society*, vii.
3. Newbigin, *Gospel in a Pluralist Society*, 14–26.
4. Bloom, *Closing of the American Mind*, 141–56.

Newbigin responds to this false dichotomy between facts and values, where especially the deliverances of science are seen as the objective "facts," and ethical claims are seen as subjective "values." He commends a critique of the doubt associated with understanding all ethical commands and virtues to be subjective. He sources this "critique of doubt" from Michael Polanyi.[5] Polanyi implies that when we undertake to doubt any statement, we do so on the basis of beliefs, which—in the act of doubting—we do not doubt. Thus knowing has to begin with an act of faith. Believing is therefore primary and doubting is secondary.[6] So those who doubt all "values" do so not on the basis of "facts," but on the basis of their own value-laden viewpoint that the ethical is a matter of opinion, while the scientific is a matter of truth.

So in critiquing the West's epistemology, Newbigin sees the need to address the West's philosophy of science. He spends time comparing the method that yields scientific understanding with the method that yields ethical understanding. He shows that there are, in fact, a number of similarities. He follows Polanyi in saying that "the authority of science is essentially traditional,"[7] just like the ethical. Thus he shows that it is simplistic to have a completely subjective view of morality and a completely objective view of science.

Newbigin is right in all this: one can potentially say to a typical Westerner, "I suspect that you don't really think *all* ethical claims are subjective values—I suspect you are very sure that child abuse and murder and so forth are objectively wrong. But if you do think that all ethics are truly subjective, and subject to doubt, how do you have such great confidence in that claim? Why not doubt that claim, rather than doubting every single moral claim that might be made?"

At this early stage of his work, Newbigin sets much of the pattern for what is to come in later chapters—for here, as throughout, he commends active engagement with those from different backgrounds from the Christian one he represents, with a goal to bring them into Christian church. He stands against the likes of George Lindbeck, who wants to treat religious doctrines as mere "rules of language."[8] Unlike Lindbeck, Newbigin's realism is such that he sees Christians compelled to hold their Christian beliefs with

---

5 Polanyi, *Personal Knowledge*, 269–71.

6. Newbigin, *Gospel in a Pluralist Society*, 19–23.

7. Polanyi, *Knowing and Being*, 66.

8. While calling Lindbeck's approach "a promising proposal," Newbigin's next sentence, quoted below, shows that his project is pitted against Lindbeck at the point of the challenge which must be presented to those who are not Christian. See Lindbeck, *Nature of Doctrine*, 32–40.

"universal intent,"[9] that is, holding them with the associated conviction that all people should believe them. For Newbigin, nothing less is required than "a resolute assault on the fundamental problem which is epistemology, the way we formulate an answer to the question, 'How do you know?'"[10]

As Newbigin comes to the heart of his proposal for actively engaging the non-Christian world, he cites a Hindu friend, reminding us of his missionary time in India: "As I read the Bible I find in it a quite unique interpretation of universal history and, therefore, a unique understanding of the human person as a responsible actor in history. You Christian missionaries have talked of the Bible as if it were simply another book of religion."[11] Newbigin emphasizes from this quote the claim of the Bible to present *universal* history. The universality of it means it must be presented to others. And the way to do this, according to Newbigin, is not to examine the Bible from the outside, but to indwell it. The Bible's structure is a narrative, so it must be rendered in narrative form, by living it out in community. This community will then operate with a "plausibility structure" which is fundamentally Christian, for the Christian narrative becomes the "frame within which one makes all decisions," which is the nature of a "plausibility structure."[12] It is such a community with such a plausibility structure which is needed to bring others into this Christian narrative. Conversely, it is only when a whole society takes on the plausibility structures of the biblical narrative that the whole society can come to Christ. Newbigin cites Athanasius's fourth-century defense of the Trinity as an "almost unbelievable" example of a time when a society's whole plausibility structure was changed.[13]

## Critique of Newbigin

Newbigin is right that we should speak beyond our own "holy huddles"[14] and seek to bring the Bible's universal message to the whole world. He is right that church communities must play a central role if this is to happen.

9. "Universal intent" is another phrase that Newbigin takes from Polanyi. See Newbigin, *Gospel in a Pluralist Society*, 34.

10. Newbigin, *Gospel in a Pluralist Society*, 24.

11. Newbigin, *Gospel in a Pluralist Society*, 80.

12. The notion of a "plausibility structure" is important to Newbigin. Plausibility structures are "patterns of belief and practice accepted within a given society, which determine which beliefs are plausible to its members and which are not." He derives the notion from Peter Berger. See Newbigin, *Gospel in a Pluralist Society*, 8; Berger, *The Sacred Canopy*, 45–51.

13. Newbigin, *Truth to Tell*, 17.

14. Newbigin uses this term. Newbigin, *Gospel in a Pluralist Society*, 242.

His appropriation of the notion of "plausibility structures" has strengths in explaining why this is so, and his appropriation of "belief with universal intent" is an important expression of what is required of the Christian. This universal mission of Christ can, however, be strengthened by employing the implications of the earlier chapters of this book.

What has been offered in my argument thus far is an understanding, particularly of revelation, that strengthens what Newbigin is saying. We have more than just an ability to give a "critique of doubt" to those who unduly divide "values" from "facts." We have more than just an ability to invite others in church communities with "plausibility structures" that commend the gospel. We can also speak to those outside of Christian belief with confidence that the moral truth they ought to live by is declared to them, by God, through his creation. Moreover, we can speak to outsiders the words of the gospel, confident that God's Spirit is attached to his evangelical revelation, so that his word will not return to him void.[15]

In the previous chapters, I have examined "legal revelation," "the expressible communication of God to all, communicating that which humanity needs to live a righteous life under the covenant of works." I have argued that it presses on all people directly, pressing on them apart from discursive reasoning or argument. This notion of a revelation grounded in the being of the world strengthens Newbigin's case. For his approach of holding beliefs with universal intent makes more sense when it is grounded in universal notions of the "good" and the "right" infused in the very being of the world. This grounding yields a power to any person speaking the truths of legal revelation to those who doubt or reject them, the power that these same truths are already pressing on every person's being through creation. This adds an ontology missing from Newbigin's presentation. When the Christian is in dialog regarding a truth of legal revelation that is disputed, the Christian always has the genuine option to speak in favor of the truth in question with universal intent, without always inviting them to the Christian community and without always putting an argument based on specific evidence.[16]

Newbigin neglects such a practical resource, partly because he overstates his case regarding "plausibility structures." On the one hand, he is

---

15. Isa 55:11.

16. Such a response is not reasoning with the unbeliever in the way William Lane Craig intends when he asserts that "it's unscriptural to refuse to reason with an unbeliever." Craig cites 1 Pet 3:15 to defend his point of view, but this verse is insufficient for his claim. It speaks of being prepared to give a reason "for the hope you have," which is not the same thing as giving a defense of any biblical truth that might be challenged. The language of giving an answer for "the hope you have" is that of explaining personal faith in the gospel, rather than defending any belief at all. The Christian is called to the former, but not necessarily the latter. See Craig, *Reasonable Faith*, 56.

correct to say with Peter Berger that there are "patterns of belief and practice accepted within a given society, which determine which beliefs are plausible to its members and which are not."[17] On television recently in Australia a young high school girl defended her sibling's "transitioning" to "male" at a young age, with language that could have come straight from a university sociology class on gender theory. That is, she employed the idea that gender was not tied to biology but a social construct assigned to her by her parents. This would have been unthinkable until recently. Clearly, the plausibility structures of Australia and the West broadly have changed, and this is a major reason why this girl spoke as she did. Yet much more than a society's "plausibility structures" frame a person's thinking in the array of moral questions they must address.

Totally at odds with the Platonic worldview, when he was speaking to the Athenians in Acts 17:16–34, what Paul proposed was that the judge of the world could become flesh, die, and be resurrected. But nevertheless, some thought, despite their own plausibility structures supported by idols, that they must hear more of this, and others even "became followers of Paul."[18] Plausibility structures alone do not determine one's mindset.

So Newbigin overemphasizes matters when he says that a plausibility structure is "by definition *the* frame within which one makes *all* decisions."[19] There are too many different moral questions in which we form viewpoints for one or even a score of plausibility structures to comprise *the* frame for *every decision*. Another very important frame is a person's past deeds and character. A thief is very likely to justify theft even within a society whose plausibility structure commends the opposite view. A person's various desires, sinful and otherwise, impact on our decisions, often in the face of the relevant plausibility structures. The state of a person's conscience also has an impact. In sum, there is far more, in the nature of the world and people that influence decisions, than just plausibility structures. My model of revelation has depicted one such additional aspect of the world and yielded one potential response when matters are disputed.

But the distinction between legal revelation and evangelical revelation not only yields practical recommendations for those defending the former, but also the latter. Newbigin's presentation can be further strengthened by the consideration that God's Spirit attaches to his gospel *word*, so that it can have effect, even when there is no gospel community present. Missionaries have to start somewhere. They need a first convert. The apostle Paul's

---

17. Newbigin, *Gospel in a Pluralist Society*, 8.
18. Acts 17:34.
19. Newbigin, *Gospel in a Pluralist Society*, 101. My emphasis.

explanation of the gospel was enough to convert Lydia, without bringing her first into a church.[20] So one must, as Newbigin says, hold our beliefs with universal intent. But one way to do this is to set forth God's evangelical revelation to unbelievers, even if we have no church yet formed with the right "plausibility structures." Newbigin's advocacy for mission to the whole world through churches with Christian "plausibility structures" is commendable. But more is needed.

So when the contested matter in discussion is one of historical matters of the gospel, for example, Jesus' death or resurrection, an unbeliever is not helped if a Christian only says, "God is pressing the truths you need to know upon you." The Christian does best when they know the Scriptures and seek to explain the apostolic witness to these events and why they were necessary. The Christian can have confidence that God's Spirit is working in the world, such that when a person examines the Scriptures, examining whether these things are so, God will be at work.

For Acts 17 declares that the noble Bereans examined the Scriptures every day to see if what Paul said was true, and οὖν, "therefore," many of them believed. It was because they were exposed to the arguments and evidence of the Scriptures, and examined them closely, that so many of them were saved. Increased exposure to Scripture, with a good heart, under God, is associated with conversion. Thus, where possible, drawing on a wide range of the teaching of Scripture as it points to Jesus and the gospel is a good goal for the Christian evangelist.

For example, if the contested claim has to do with God's existence, it is wise to note that answers focusing on Jesus revealing God are more likely to move towards gospel themes compared with answers to do with the science of origins of the universe. The latter has its place, but the former is more likely to lead to unpacking the message of the gospel, and therefore likely to be more fruitful.[21]

In sum, in coming from the direction of a theology of revelation, my model gives the Christian more advice on how to confidently set forth Christ in a pluralist environment. Newbigin's context is that he is writing to a Christian audience, understanding that Christianity is slipping to the margins in the West. The question is whether that means we should turn down our volume, and Newbigin is saying by no means—we should keep the volume loud. He is right in this, but more can be said in support of his claim. I have presented an additional basis for keeping the volume up,

---

20. Acts 16:14.

21. For more detail, and practical examples, see Chapman, *Know and Tell the Gospel*, 132–36.

and additional ways to present biblical truth, grounded in the distinction between evangelical and legal revelation.

As a final comment, before considering McGrath, it is worth observing that the postmodern mood that Newbigin contests arguably has shifted to become less dominant in the twenty-first-century West, forty years after Newbigin. The public has polarized toward several absolutes—against child abuse; for "rights"; for and against climate change; for the dignity of minorities; for the preservation of my nation-state; and so on. Although incontestable reasons for these convictions can never be given nor found, which is the legacy of postmodernism, the convictions remain viscerally self-evident to people. The somewhat shrill and aggressive moral discourse of our time would seem precisely to support my claim that moral truth "presses in" on us all. This change of zeitgeist may deserve further exploration.[22] With that note, it is time then to turn to Alister McGrath.

## ALISTER McGRATH

Alister McGrath is a former atheist converted to Christianity, with a background in both physical and biological sciences. As a result, he is aware of a number of the rationalistic challenges atheism brings against Christianity and is astute in discussing the implications of science for Christian faith. Yet McGrath also has the strength that he is quite sensitive to the cultural changes that have taken place in the West in the past fifty or so years and their implications for evangelism and apologetics. So in his book *Mere Apologetics*, McGrath not only spends time on the specific arguments that have featured in apologetic literature, both ancient and contemporary; he also spends a lot of time discussing the nature of our present culture and how the nature of culture should impact the way a Christian contends for the Christian faith.

## MERE APOLOGETICS

Early in his book, McGrath describes the present period as "postmodern" in outlook, in contrast to the "modern" period which preceded it, which he dates at around 1750–1960. Following Vanhoozer, he outlines four aspects of this culture: First, denying the notion of universal rationality. Second, seeing truth as "a compelling story told by persons in positions of power

---

22. The observations of this paragraph are thanks to Andrew Cameron, in his marking of the thesis from which this work derives.

in order to perpetuate their way of seeing and organizing the natural and social world." Third, an incredulous stance towards any presentation of universal history. Fourth, the conviction that there is no universal answer to the question of human identity.[23] His aim is not to critique modernity or postmodernity, but to take them as cultural "givens," assuming that both have strengths and weaknesses.[24] He does not reflect an approach of any of the "schools" of apologetics, but seeks to equip the reader to develop their own method as well as to answer specific questions. So his advice includes the need to understand the faith, understand the audience, communicate clearly, find points of contact with the audience, present the whole gospel, and practice answering questions.[25] He takes general principles from the way Peter and Paul vary their presentation of the gospel according to the changes in their audience. So, drawing on Acts 2, 17, and 24–26, the three principles he finds are these: address the specific audience, identify authorities that carry weight with the audience, and use lines of argument that will carry weight with the audience.[26]

McGrath underlines that there are elements of Christianity that do not need to be proven: "To demonstrate the reasonableness of faith does not mean proving every article of faith. Rather, it means being able to demonstrate that there are good grounds for believing these articles are trustworthy and reliable."[27] He points to C. S. Lewis as a great example of this: "C. S. Lewis's remarkable success as an apologist was partly due to his ability to offer 'a positive exhibition of the force of Christian ideas, morally, imaginatively, and rationally.'"[28] McGrath rightly points out that the waning of rationalism in Western culture has made the use of arguments less important than it was and has "created a context in which other aspects of the Christian faith need to be recognized—above all, its powerful imaginative, moral, and aesthetic appeal."[29] In particular, he points to a difficulty in seeing Christian apologetics "simply in terms of developing effective arguments designed to persuade people that the Christian faith is true." He calls this approach "not well-grounded in the Bible," since God is the "secure

---

23. McGrath, *Mere Apologetics*, 33–34; Vanhoozer, "Condition of Postmodernity," 4–23.

24. McGrath, *Mere Apologetics*, 31.

25. McGrath, *Mere Apologetics*, 35–38.

26. McGrath, *Mere Apologetics*, 67–68.

27. McGrath, *Mere Apologetics*, 79.

28. Here McGrath takes his analysis of C. S. Lewis from Austin Farrer. McGrath, *Mere Apologetics*, 79; Farrer, "In His Image," 344–45.

29. McGrath, *Mere Apologetics*, 128.

base."³⁰ Instead, McGrath offers five "ways into Christianity," the last three of which have an increasing appeal now after the age of modernity. They are explanation, argument, story, images, and the way Christians live and embody their faith.³¹

Not only in his apologetics book, but especially in his other writings, McGrath has spent time drawing parallels between the way science works and the way biblical Christianity can be commended to outsiders. So he draws on American scientist and philosopher Charles Peirce to point out that one of the three main types of scientific explanation, abduction, is a fine tool in the Christian apologist's hand. For the Christian, like the scientist can argue "to the best explanation."³² The Christian can ask questions like, "What must be true if we are to explain what is observed?" and "What big picture of reality offers the best fit to what is actually observed in our experience?"³³ This was the kind of reasoning that brought C. S. Lewis to faith.³⁴ McGrath quotes Lewis in this regard, who reflecting on his life before conversion says, "Nearly all that I loved I believed to be imaginary; nearly all that I believed to be real I thought grim and meaningless."³⁵

### Critique of McGrath

McGrath offers an appealing breadth of recommendation and insight for the Christian who hopes to bring an outsider towards Christianity. He provides a greater grounding in reality than Newbigin for confident evangelism and apologetic discourse, reflecting well that the "big picture" of the "Christian faith" rains from the sky as a "meteoric shower of facts."³⁶ His set of recommendations for engagement is wide because he sees a great width in the way God communicates—not just rationally, but morally, aesthetically, through imagination, story, image, and more. He mentions, briefly, but helpfully, that an important part of the context of reaching out to unbelievers is that "human nature" is "wounded and damaged by sin," so that "we are not capable of seeing things as they really are." This enables him, more than Newbigin, to rightly emphasize why the Christian must point outside of

---

30. McGrath, *Mere Apologetics*, 137.
31. McGrath, *Mere Apologetics*, 154–55.
32. McGrath, *Mere Apologetics*, 110; Peirce, *Collected Papers*, 5:189.
33. McGrath, Mere Apologetics, 82.
34. McGrath, *Mere Apologetics*, 82.
35. McGrath, *Mere Apologetics*, 137; Lewis, *Surprised by Joy*, 170.
36. McGrath takes this image from American poet Edna St. Vincent Millay. McGrath, *Mere Apologetics*, 93; St. Vincent Millay, "Upon This Age," 140.

himself and outside of the church community to Jesus as our Savior.[37] In his apologetic work, he barely touches on Newbigin's theme of the importance of the church community embodying the truth, and this may be a defect. But he ends up with a praxis that is stronger, for its ontological grounding is stronger.

Yet it can be strengthened still further by taking on board the model of revelation I have been propounding. For McGrath fails to clearly differentiate between the *distinctively Christian* truths that he defends and truths shared with other worldviews that he also defends. That is, he fails to be sufficiently clear about the relative importance of his different arguments. One way to see this is at a juncture in *Mere Apologetics* where he denigrates apologetic methods focused solely on developing arguments for "the Christian faith."[38] In defending this point, he argues that the Bible has *God* as a "secure base,"[39] by which he seems to mean God's existence and nature are not argued for in the Bible, as though one might properly doubt his existence. But of course, the fact that God is a "secure base," thereby not needing arguments to defend his existence, does not imply that "Christian faith" is the same kind of "secure base," apologetically speaking. And indeed "God" and "the Christian faith" are treated very differently in the Bible. While God himself is not argued for in the Bible, as though it might be a fair thing to doubt his existence, the "Christian faith" is very much argued for. The apostles appealed to fulfilled prophecy, miracles, the coming of the Spirit at Pentecost, and Jesus' resurrection as evidence that he was the Christ.[40] McGrath would acknowledge this distinction if it were placed in front of him, yet he makes the typical apologetic writer's mistake of generalizing about apologetic method across every kind of Christian truth because he does not have the tools to differentiate clearly that this present work has provided.

One implication of this oversight is that McGrath does not see how many of the Bible's claims he could also treat as a "secure base," in addition to God. He does not see that he could downplay not only the use of arguments for God's existence, but arguments for all the elements of "legal revelation." That is, he would be right to also downplay the use of arguments against stealing or lying, or sexual immorality, or the fact that there are possessions, that there are two sexes, male and female, and so on. He could call these also

---

37. McGrath, *Mere Apologetics*, 45–46.
38. McGrath, *Mere Apologetics*, 137.
39. McGrath, *Mere Apologetics*, 137.
40. The phrasing here is adapted from Craig, "Classical Apologetics," 41.

a "secure base," from an epistemological perspective.[41] For all these elements press on us through creation, and the Bible often assumes them.

Another implication of his oversight is that in his extensive discussion of the relation between science and "faith," he does not identify the relative importance of the different arguments he is making, or of the truths he is defending. This is a problem exacerbated somewhat by the fact that his expertise is in the area of science rather than historical apologetics. So he spends little if any time on the latter, despite it being more important, and much more time on the former, despite it being less important. It is less important, because in dealing with science, McGrath is typically defending truths that people can know apart from special revelation and have come to know across all times and cultures. Yet he is not spending nearly as much time defending those elements of Christian truth that are only able to be known through the historical testimony of the apostles and prophets, through the Scriptures. This would be fine if he explained the relative importance of the two, but he does not. In view of this, let us consider in a little more detail some of his writing on science.

## McGrath on Science

It is a strength that McGrath, like Newbigin, spends time demonstrating the parallels between the scientific approach to truth and the ways Christian belief can be commended to outsiders. His book *Surprised by Meaning* explains the scientific use of the concept of "abduction"—inference to the best fit[42]—and employs that to argue for Christianity in a variety of ways: The fine-tuning of the universe to life is a data point that bolsters Christianity as the best explanation for reality, since the God of Christianity can be expected to have fine-tuned the universe for life, whereas the chaotic randomness implied by atheism does not fit that data point well.[43] Likewise, the data of world wars and tyrants bolsters Christianity as the best explanation for the universe because Christianity has a strong doctrine of sin which explains such things, whereas notions of history as pure progress do not fit this data

---

41. There are certain kinds of arguments for truths of "legal revelation" in the Bible. For example, descriptions of the folly of the idol-maker and idol-worshiper are a certain kind of argument against idolatry. Yet these do not argue in such a way as to acknowledge that one might be excused for believing in idols or worshiping them. See, for example, Isa 44:19–20.

42. McGrath, *Surprised by Meaning*, 10.

43. McGrath, *Surprised by Meaning*, 58–65.

well.[44] Again, the fact that scholars of biology find that some form of "end goal" or "teleology" is fundamental to their discipline points to Christianity as a better explanation of the world than the undirected universe implied by atheism, since Christianity inherently believes in a God who does move things to an end goal, whereas atheism does not.[45] The fact that Darwin and his main interpreter, Huxley, believed that evolution does not rule out inherent purpose in the world points to Christianity as no weaker an explanatory worldview at this point than atheism.[46] McGrath presents these arguments as various ways to contend, especially against militant scientific atheism, for Christian faith, in an abductive manner.

Yet *Surprised by Meaning* could benefit from a proper application of the distinction between "evangelical revelation" and "legal revelation" and its implications for the relative importance of different parts of the Christian message. For in so doing he would have been able to more clearly identify the relative accessibility of different kinds of truth, as well as the role of different truths, in saving or condemning sinners, or simply contributing to scientific or other human knowledge.

It is worth noting that scientific knowledge is more like "evangelical revelation" than "legal revelation." For neither the historical truths of the gospel nor the deliverances of science can be known apart from them being set forth and explained. No remote tribal community can grasp the Christian gospel without a missionary going and telling them about Jesus, just as no remote tribal community can grasp, say, the botanical characteristics of New Zealand without someone knowledgeable in that area explaining it to them.

But more importantly, when *Surprised by Meaning* is viewed as a whole, it is noteworthy that the book, even in the chapter devoted to speaking about Christianity, does not discuss Jesus' life, death, or resurrection. Again, this may be because it is more the historian than the natural scientist who has the tools to explore the claims of evangelical revelation focused on Christ. McGrath with his background as a natural scientist is speaking in his area of expertise and should not be faulted for that. But the book presents as tying science to *Christianity*, not just theism. It seems that *Surprised by Meaning* is in fact a book best described as showing the consistency of science with *theism*, or with *legal revelation*. The book's subtitle is *Science, Faith, and How We Make Sense of Things*. One suspects that the term "faith" in the subtitle might be there rather than "Christianity" because it is more

---

44. McGrath, *Surprised by Meaning*, 82–90.
45. McGrath, *Surprised by Meaning*, 74–81.
46. McGrath, *Surprised by Meaning*, 74–81.

theism than Christianity that is discussed. But for Christians, "faith" is trust *in Jesus*. And yet the book says very little about Jesus. The model of revelation here depicted would help McGrath to untangle this.

It is not that McGrath should, for instance, move to compare different theisms to underscore the greater plausibility of Christian theism over other theisms as a reasonable explanation of the physical world. It is clear that this will draw up short of acknowledgment of Christ as Lord and God. McGrath could, on the one hand, do more to underscore the plausibility of *Christian theism* by spending some time in historical apologetics, perhaps connecting this with the way the Old Testament pointed forward to the nature of the coming Christ. But this would be a different book, outside of McGrath's expertise. More plausibly, what would significantly strengthen *Surprised by Meaning* is an acknowledgment that it is a defense of a small subset of Christian claims, a subset which is shared by some non-Christian worldviews, a subset less important than the claims that are distinctively Christian. It would strengthen McGrath's book to acknowledge that the majority of truths being defended in it have been held by those who have had great access to Christian and scientific teachings, *as well as held by those who have no access to Christian and scientific teachings*, an observation which should point to the limitations of the book in defending Christianity itself. This would frame the project properly, rather than presenting as a defense of "faith," implying Christian faith.

Nevertheless, like with Newbigin, McGrath very much advocates the "keeping the volume up" approach as we engage others in our pluralist society with the truth of Jesus. And again, like with Newbigin, I have shown how my proposed model of revelation strengthens that case even further.

## ARGUMENTATION STRATEGY

To conclude this chapter, I wish to propose an argumentation strategy, which can be derived from my distinction between legal and evangelical revelation. In considering this argumentation strategy, imagine a dialog between a Christian and another person disputing or calling into question some biblical truth-claim. It is in that context that I propose five elements to guide the Christian conversationalist:

1. The first element is to understand that one's argumentation strategy should differ depending on the nature of the particular biblical truth-claim being contested.

2. The second element is to dialog without ever feeling compelled to present arguments for the truths of legal revelation which rely on localized evidence, or complicated argumentation.

3. The third element is to see that arguments in favor of the truths of legal revelation[47] have a disagreeable element which rises in proportion to their dependence on complicated argumentation and localized evidence.[48]

4. The fourth element is to actively defend those elements of evangelical revelation that are not universally available[49] to know.

5. The fifth element is to aim to show the connection of the contested truth-claim to the major themes of the gospel of Jesus.

Elements 1, 2, 4, and 5 have already been considered in the discussion above. It remains to consider element 3.

If every person is already without excuse, and subject to God's judgment for failing to live according to a truth of legal revelation, they do not *need* a deductive proof of that truth. They do not lack a cogent presentation of this truth, since God is pressing it upon them already through his created order, as previous chapters have maintained. It may well be loving to present a proof of this truth from premises the person already accepts. This might be a good course of action and an important thing to do. But if no such proof comes to mind, or if no answer to an attack on this truth is forthcoming, or if the Christian simply feels it not the right context, the Christian is under no obligation to give one. This is because God is already giving a much better "proof" through his creation, both through what is pressing on each person from outside and through the inner construction of each person.

As already discussed above, the Christian could merely say words to the effect of, "I think God is pressing this truth upon us through the way he made the world, but none of us receives this like we should." This could be an opportunity for the Christian to discuss with the interlocutor what seems self-evident to them and to affirm it where possible, stating how Christian thought accounts for it. In other words, a place for discussion of

47. Recall here that legal revelation is defined as "the expressible communication of God to all, communicating that which humanity needs to live a righteous life under the covenant of works." This includes the "God-ward" aspects of revelation—our responsibilities towards God and the things we need to know about him to live rightly.

48. That is, evidence which can only be accessed in a specific place or time, such as historical evidence.

49. Not universally available in that knowledge of these truths relies on localized evidence or complicated argumentation.

shared agreements about what "presses in" upon all of us is an entailment of this work.

But my substantive point here is that failure to reason directly on a particular contested element of "legal revelation" is not only a genuine option to consider in apologetic discourse, but may indeed be the best answer in the circumstance. For such an answer avoids a disagreeable element that is present whenever a Christian argues for such truths with complicated argumentation or localized evidence, that is, evidence which can only be accessed in a specific place or time, such as historical evidence. If a dialog partner is newly convinced of a truth of legal revelation through a complicated argument, or by appeal to localized evidence, this person may plausibly conclude that others have an excuse for not accepting that truth of legal revelation. This would be the excuse that many in the world lack either the intellectual ability to understand the argument or that they do not have the relevant evidence available to them. Thus, there is always a risk in giving such arguments that a person is led into a combination of new truth *and* new error, the error being to deny that God justly judges people when they are ignorant of legal revelation, or to deny that God justly judges people when they exhibit moral culpability connected to such ignorance.

This risk rises with the level of complexity in the argument, for the more complex it is, the more likely a person convinced by it will conclude that others have an excuse for not grasping it—the excuse that they or others are not smart enough. A claim of universal significance, like the gospel of salvation, cannot be elitist based on intellectual capacity.

Alternately, the risk also rises with the degree to which evidence used in the argument is localized, and therefore not universally available. For the more the evidence is localized, the more a person convinced by the evidence might reasonably conclude that many have an excuse for not believing in this truth, namely the excuse that they do not have access to the evidence in question. Hence, as element 3 of my argumentation strategy proposes, arguments in favor of the truths of legal revelation have this disagreeable element which rises in proportion to their dependence on complicated argumentation and localized evidence. It should be stressed that this critique does not apply to the gospel because the claim is not that all people everywhere ought to live according to the gospel, by trusting and following Jesus. That is a false claim—people who have never heard the gospel do not need to make an excuse for not believing in a man of whom they have never heard. It is only for legal revelation that I make the claim that all people ought to live according to it. Therefore it is only regarding legal revelation that arguments depending on localized evidence have a disagreeable element.

## CONCLUSION

I have shown in this chapter the different ways in which the proposed model of revelation yields practical and liveable applications and how it strengthens the case for a robust outreach with the Christian gospel, even in a pluralist environment with all its different faiths and none.

Newbigin's account can be strengthened by seeing that it lacks a grounding in the being of reality. My more subtle account of God's activity in revelation bypasses the plausibility trap that Newbigin seeks to overcome, shifting the gospel into a community, within the world, that lives out the gospel. In my account, revelation is still a form of manifest "evidence." While bypassing rationalism, my account still sets forth a revelation that is expressible, in both its legal and evangelical forms. This means that the expression of both evangelical, and even legal, revelation can be understood as a form of apologetic argument.

McGrath's account is strengthened by bringing a precision to his definition of "Christian faith." By utilizing the distinction between legal and evangelical revelation, one can see that many of his arguments are in fact arguments for elements of legal revelation, and therefore of lesser importance, and on a less stable footing, than arguments for the gospel.

In addition to the substantial resources already offered by Newbigin and McGrath, I have added a five-element argumentation strategy. It remains only for a final chapter to take stock of the ground covered so far.

# Chapter 7

# Conclusion

In my first chapter, I proffered the question which is the focus for this work: if neither general revelation nor natural law are accessible to people reliably, how can God justly judge them for their ignorance and hold them morally culpable for failing to live according to revelation they cannot reliably access?

To understand this question and the terminology, I gave a brief definition and history of the terms general revelation and natural law. I take general revelation to mean "truths about God that can be known through nature." I take natural law to mean "truths about ethical universals that can be known through nature." A noteworthy element of chapter 2 is the finding that modern scholarship of apologetic method universally fails to grasp that matters of ethics should be treated differently from matters of history. Thus, imprecisely defined concepts of God's revelation remain to this day and yield a discourse in theology and apologetics which is not as gospel-shaped as it should be.

But more importantly for my ongoing argument, I build new terminology on the back of Luther's duality between a condemning "legal knowledge" and a saving "evangelical knowledge" of God. Luther's term "legal knowledge" has the strength that it allows for a fusion of general revelation and natural law under one heading. Yet a weakness in Luther's expression is his use of the term "knowledge," for Luther wrongly sees "legal knowledge" as subjectively received by all people. The term "legal revelation" is more suitable terminology, for it captures the notion that there is a body of content that God is conveying, even if it is not reliably received by sinful humanity.

Thus, I propose a key distinction for this present argument: that between legal and evangelical revelation, legal revelation is "the expressible communication of God to all, communicating that which humanity needs to live a righteous life under the covenant of works"; evangelical revelation is "the expressible communication of God, communicating that which humanity needs to live a righteous life under the covenant of grace."

This new terminology has the advantage of treating *both* the "theological" and the "ethical" as part of that which God communicates generally. This makes sense because the theological and the ethical *together* comprise the law communicated to all, sufficient for us to adjudicate, and sufficient for God to condemn our moral failure. The overlap between the theological and ethical is clear in that God's character implies ethical imperatives, and ethical imperatives rest on realities, including the theological. The term "legal" denotes this key function of that revelation, that a sufficient *law* is given to all. Correspondingly, the term "evangelical" denotes the key function of that revelation, that a *gospel* is given, sufficient to save. This distinction in terminology is grounded in an important epistemic distinction: that on the one hand, there is a legal revelation to which all people have always had access. This is distinct, on the other hand, from the "evangelical" revelation which is accessible only when people hear the good news proclaimed, news which has been spreading from its source in Jerusalem two thousand years ago.

Thus, I put my first major proposition, that making this distinction is important in answering the major question of the book. Recall that the question is: if neither general revelation nor natural law are accessible to people reliably, how can God justly judge them for their ignorance and hold them morally culpable for failing to live according to revelation they cannot reliably access? My distinction helps to answer the question because it simplifies. In treating general revelation and natural law as a single entity—"legal revelation"—I have a question about one entity, instead of a question about two. This new terminology simplifies the problem, as well as depicting reality better than previous terminology.

In chapter 3, I stated the proposal of the book as a series of propositions. In addition to the first proposition, a second proposition was added. I propose that the broadest answer to the problem is "it is humanity's fault not God's that legal revelation is not accessible to people reliably." Five realities support this claim: *First, that each element of legal revelation's content is designed for "short and easy"*[1] *reception,* so that it is not God's fault for making legal revelation too complicated or difficult to receive. It is not too complicated or difficult to receive. *Second, that each element of legal revelation is communicated universally and continually,* so that God cannot be accused of making it only available in certain localized times or places. This is saying that a part of my definition of "legal revelation," namely its universality, is a key reality in defending God against the charge that he condemns unjustly. *Third, that all people internalize an ethical map approximating legal revelation, but we do so with flaws*—flaws that are culpable, with blame resting on us as individuals, and on others who have influenced us, but not with God. *Fourth, that problems in humanity's disposition, which hinder the reception of legal revelation, are humanity's fault,* since Adam and Eve could wholly receive it pre-fall. While the third reality blames us for our flawed internalization of legal revelation, this fourth reality blames Adam and our other forebears for our fallen nature. That is, Adam, and those who have followed him down the centuries, bear blame for our current nature, which is such that it cannot internalize legal revelation reliably. This endemic inability is God's just judgment on us for Adam's sin and for our other forebears' sin, and for our individual sin. *Fifth, that God's continued communication of his legal revelation is manifest,* seen in the fact that each element of legal revelation is still being received through nature by many people, pointing to the blame resting on us, rather than God, for his revelation not being reliably received.

My exegesis of Romans 1:18—2:1 and 2:14–15 shows that the apostle Paul expressed himself in ways consistent with these propositions. Romans 1:18—2:1 was chosen as a passage commonly understood to discuss general revelation, meaning approximately truths about God that can be known through nature. Romans 2:14–15 was chosen as a passage commonly understood to discuss natural law, meaning approximately truths about ethical universals that can be known through nature. In support of the various subsections of proposition 2, my exegesis was such that I drew the following conclusions:

> i. The typical "short and easy" human reception of legal revelation is undergirded by the notion of our being "without excuse" (1:20; 2:1), since if reception of legal revelation were "long and complicated," the time and difficulty to receive it would present viable excuses for not living according to them. Likewise, the understanding that some of the things of the law are written on each human heart (2:14–15)

---

1. The phrase "short and easy" was taken from Samuel Hopkins. "Immediate and accessible" is a potential alternative expression.

undergirds "short and easy" reception of legal revelation, since that which is written on our heart is easily accessed.

ii. God's *universal* communication of his legal revelation is buttressed by seeing 1:18–32 as referring to *all* humanity, and 2:14–15 as referring to *all* Gentile hearts. Legal revelation's *continued* dissemination is supported in the temporal phrase ἀπό κτίσεως κόσμου, "since the creation of the world," in 1:20.

iii. The partial, flawed internalization of legal revelation is supported by understanding the aorist, past time of "they knew God" (1:21) as referring to Adam and Eve, but not to all people today. For were the passage referring to all people *today*, and stated that "all *know* God," rather than stating that "they *knew* God," it could plausibly be taken as a full internalization of a knowledge of God, rather than a partial, flawed one. But this is contrary to the past time aorist tense that is actually in the passage. Even if this reading of the tense in 1:21 is rejected, a partial and flawed internalization by us all suffices to sustain Paul's point, as the whole of this book attests. Partial internalization of legal revelation is also supported by reading 2:15 as saying only *some* of the requirements of the law are written on their hearts, namely, those requirements they do by nature (2:14), which is not all of them. If *all* of the requirements of the law were written on our hearts, this would not be a *partial, flawed* internalization of the law, but a complete and accurate one.

iv. Humanity's culpability for our inability to reliably receive legal revelation is undergirded by reading 1:21–32 as an historical narrative commencing with Adam and Eve and concluding in the present. Such a reading pays close attention to the tenses used in the passage, moving as it does from aorist tense, past time (1:21), to present tense, present time (1:32). This reading sees the passage vindicating God by showing how in various ways humanity through the ages has done things to deserve the judgment which consists in its sinful desires, shameful lusts, depraved mind, and other evil dispositions (1:24, 26, 28–32). This is more plausible than seeing each individual, *qua individual* as entirely responsible for their fallen nature. For some of our evil dispositions clearly derive from the parents and the society that raised us, as well as from the genetics which we inherited from our forebears.

v. The notion that God has *manifestly* continued to communicate his legal revelation through all of history is underscored in 1:20 by the present passives νοούμενα, "being understood," and καθορᾶται, "have been seen," as well as in the present tense verb ἐνδείκνυνται, "they show," of 2:15. In the latter case, it is the continued existence, over time, of Gentiles who do the requirements of the law by nature, which shows the continued effective communication by God of his legal revelation.

In light of this exegesis, it is a fair conclusion that my reading of Romans 1 and 2 is consistent with my main propositions broadly speaking and consistent with the proposal to combine the concepts of general revelation and natural law into a single concept of "legal revelation."

In chapter 4, I focused on the concept of *internalization*, for the third subpoint above utilizes this concept. The plausibility of my use of this concept is shown by introducing the category of anthropology, focused on human perceptions of objects, informed by the language of object relations theory. The overall proposal is that the "projection" and "introjection" of psychoanalysis might be understood as the "internalization" which I described in my exegesis of Romans. Key proposals of object relations theory are that we "introject" external objects, so that they become part of ourselves, and "project" aspects of ourselves onto external objects. Another important proposal is the notion of "splitting": especially in early stages of development, an infant splits both the self and external objects into "good" and "bad," unable at first to cope with a single breast or a mother that is at the same time "good" and "bad."

Under the umbrella of "projection and introjection as internalization," I present nine claims which together comprise my model:

i. Just as a child internalizes images of other objects such as their parents, they also internalize an image of God.

ii. All of these introjected images imperfectly map the reality, which is why the child keeps altering them as they develop.

iii. In addition to God himself, images of the ethics of how God and others ought to be treated are also internalized.

iv. The accuracy of this ethical mapping has no correlation to the intelligence of the subject.

v. This object and relational mapping can be described as partly intuitive,[2] in the sense that not all of it is expressible or even conscious.

vi. The internalization of God as an object is a phenomenon which draws on experiences in the world such as those with the parent, or the wished-for or imagined parent, or the grandeur of nature.

vii. It is common for people to project elements of the self onto God, crediting God with human desires and traits that he may or may not actually have.

viii. As the child grows, the internalization of "legal revelation" can also draw on various experiences that God himself has designed for that purpose. These include corporate and private prayer, praise of God, and hearing Scripture read, taught, applied, considered, and explained, experience of ritual, such as the scriptural sacraments, and more.

ix. Ethical and theological claims made by a child's family and community are likely to be believed at first by the child, but in time, an adult will revise their conscious and unconscious mappings in accordance with their experience, desires, actions, character, and more.

With this model in place, it can be plausibly suggested that an objectively flawed mapping of legal revelation might exist in us all, such that this flawed mapping is our fault. For just as the theorized category of splitting has plausibility, so by parallel has the claim that we might internalize object images in a faulty way, partly to aid our ability to act or think in ways we want, partly to avoid the anxiety or fear associated with acknowledging reality, and for other reasons. These suppressions plausibly arise from our sinful motives, rendering them our fault. In this model, it is unnecessary to undergird such culpability with a claim that each person knows on some level that God is there, for in the model, internalization of external objects is not always accurate or reliable. This model plausibly explains the world in various ways. It explains the universal religious impulse, for in the model, the reality of God's existence and character objectively presses on all, in parallel to the way our mother's existence and character press upon us. It explains polytheism, for the model explains how we might through our fear and selfishness distort the power of God by inaccurately internalizing multiple, less powerful gods, rather than the one true all-powerful God. The model gives us ways to speak about our flawed reception of legal revelation

2. By "intuitive" I mean "formed apart from the processes of discursive reason."

in dynamic rather than static ways, based as it is on the dynamic object relations theory. The model outlined adds plausibility to my overall case because it is grounded in a theory with roots in experimental data.

In chapter 5, I sought to demonstrate that in the light of study of key philosophical and ethical ideas pertinent to the topic, my argument grows in plausibility. I propose that the obligatory, that is, "the right"—being best understood at its deepest level as obedience to God's commands—is either expressed concretely in the words of his prophets and Scripture or expressed by implication in the created moral order. This infusion of "the right" in the created order undergirds the truth that each element of legal revelation is communicated *universally*. It is *because* every person has commonality of design—*because* of the order wherein humans are of a common kind, with common ends—that every element of legal revelation can apply to every human. It is because the right is implied in our creation, *and* expressible, that people from every language and culture can come to grasp its various elements and express them.

I also propose a partial theological voluntarism, with some but not all of God's commands regarded as necessary.[3] This bolsters the plausibility of a universal legal revelation reflected in the commands of Scripture. For this voluntarism enables us to say, for example, that some of the food laws of the Old Testament could have been different in detail than they are while still serving their purpose. The seemingly arbitrary nature of some of them need not be taken as evidence that a universal legal revelation is unsupportable in Scripture.

I take the position that there are human faculties which must exist in every person, such as the will, conscience, self-consciousness, rationality, emotion, language comprehension, and moral "vision," though these faculties may be damaged by sin, or otherwise. Since the fall, these faculties have kept their form, character, nature, set, and direction as "human faculties," though each is sullied by the fall. "Legal revelation" addresses our whole person, addressing every faculty directly with its own instruction-set. Since every faculty is addressed, a person can be held culpable for sinful responses, no matter the faculty from which they stem. Note that this depiction of "legal revelation" is such that, outside the context of this present work, others may prefer to use alternative terms such as "natural accountability" or "created awareness."

I define the content of natural law such that it includes expressible commands, virtues, vices, and truths that must be understood to grasp all

---

3. Recall that a necessary command is one such that it holds in every possible world that God could have created.

of these, with content spanning both the "ethical" and the "theological." My depiction of natural law is such that it must include the "theological," thus becoming "legal revelation" as I have defined it, rather than that which has been traditionally styled as natural law. This is in tune with the approach of this book, in merging natural law and general revelation. I hold to a fixity in this natural law, such that God has faithfully continued to communicate his legal revelation across the ages.

My position on how one knows the natural law is that it cannot be found solely in concepts of pure reason, for reason cannot easily reach all of the ethical categories to which legal revelation speaks. Yet every individual element of natural law is able to be discerned, apart from Scripture, by some. For this undergirds the claim that no one has an excuse. Yet many are unable to discern specific elements because of their past deeds, or their society's influence, or for other reasons. No one can reliably discern the whole of the legal revelation. This position fits well with the joint proposition that humanity is to blame for our unreliable reception of legal revelation and that God has continued to communicate this revelation reliably.

Finally, I propose accepting an ethical intuitionism. This is the view that ethical principles are knowable non-inferentially and intuitively. Such a position undergirds the view that legal revelation may be internalized in "short and easy" fashion, so that the excuse is not available to anyone that the content of legal revelation was too difficult to grasp.

If my formulation in answering the problem is to be considered plausible, then one would need to see how it impacts upon our engagement with the secular world. To do so, I considered two leading figures in the modern era, Lesslie Newbigin and Alister McGrath. In chapter 6, I showed that Newbigin's approach is to say that we need to hold our beliefs with universal intent even in the face of a pluralist society. But what I have been saying grounds this approach ontologically, providing greater confidence to the Christian. Both the apologist and the evangelist can be more confident when they understand that their beliefs are grounded in universal notions of the "good" and the "right" infused in the very being of the world. I showed that McGrath's writing, especially on scientific matters, fails to differentiate adequately between distinctively Christian truths and those truths shared with other worldviews. He would be helped in seeing clearly the relative importance of his arguments if he made more use of the distinction between "legal" and "evangelical" revelation, as I have been presenting. For in so doing he would have been able to more clearly see the relative accessibility of different kinds of truth, as well as the role and relative importance of different truths, in saving or condemning sinners, or simply in contributing to scientific or other human knowledge.

The plausibility of my proposal is also strengthened by its practical and pastoral feasibility. To that end, I propose a five-element argumentation strategy for a Christian in dialog with another person calling into question some biblical truth-claim:

i. The first element is to understand that one's argumentation strategy should differ depending on the nature of the particular biblical truth-claim being contested.

ii. The second element is to dialog without ever feeling compelled to present arguments for the truths of legal revelation which rely on localized evidence, or complicated argumentation.

iii. The third element is to see that arguments in favor of the truths of legal revelation have a disagreeable element which rises in proportion to their dependence on complicated argumentation and localized evidence.

iv. The fourth element is to actively defend those elements of evangelical revelation that are not universally available to know.

v. The fifth element is to aim to show the connection of the contested truth-claim to the major themes of the gospel of Jesus.

This brings us to the very end of the matter. The question was, if neither general revelation nor natural law are accessible to people reliably, how can God justly judge them for their ignorance and hold them morally culpable for failing to live according to revelation they cannot reliably access? Let me answer in a single paragraph:

No one can complain on the Last Day that God communicated insufficient "ethical" or "theological" reality to them, because the scope of God's revelation, through his creation, *is* sufficient for living a blameless life. No one can complain that this revelation is too intellectually difficult to internalize, since it may be internalized in "short and easy" fashion. No one can complain that the relevant revelation was not universally available, since God has continued to convey it through all of history, to all people. This is manifest, since for every truth of legal revelation, people can always be found who have rightly internalized that truth, apart from the Scriptures. The fault lies with humanity that God's revelation is unreliably accessible to us, because our failure to reliably internalize it is sourced in our self-centeredness, our anxieties, our fears, our past sinful deeds, as well our fallen nature, which is humanity's fault rather than God's. Developmental psychology helps us see how this is plausibly so, for it has provided a model, based on empirical observation, of the way we come to grasp important concepts and realities from the earliest stages of life, in "short and easy" fashion. According to this model, from the youngest age, people seek after true representations of reality, and yet, for culpable reasons such as fear, anxiety, and self-centeredness, our internal representations of external reality are skewed and unreliable. Such a psychological model may be extended to the "ethical" and "theological" realm—on the assumption that God is willing to reveal himself through parts of the created order such as parent figures and their disciplines. This answer, speaking as it does in the same way of "ethical" and "theological" reality, depends on a fusing of the concepts of general revelation and natural law. This is plausible because God's self-revelation has ethical implications and because of the commonality of function, that failure to live according to *either* general revelation or natural law is sufficient to deserve condemnation.

The question I have attempted to answer is not straightforward. It touches on a wide variety of theological areas and disciplines, and much has been left unsaid or unconsidered that could have been addressed. A proper answer must seek to engage a wide array of disciplines, which I have attempted. I have sought to show on many levels how God can be the *just* judge of all the world, who holds us all responsible for our choices regardless of our sense of theological or moral insight. This is, in a sense, an unwelcome topic in a pluralistic and atheistic era. But when we grasp God's justice and hold it high, we can then also hold his mercy high, praising him all the more for his grand rescue of sinners through his Son. May the glory go to him.

# Bibliography

Achtemeier, Paul. *Romans*. Atlanta: John Knox, 1985.
Adams, Robert Merrihew. "A Modified Divine Command Theory of Ethical Wrongness." In *The Virtue of Faith and Other Essays in Philosophical Theology*, 97–122. Oxford: Oxford University Press, 1987.
———. "A New Divine Command Theory." In *Ethics: Essential Readings in Moral Theory*, edited by George Sher, 9:135–44. New York: Routledge, 2012.
Alexander of Hales, et al. *Summa Theologica*. Vol. 4. Quaracchi: Editiones Collegii S. Bonaventurae, 1924.
Aquinas, Thomas. "Commentary on Psalm 18." Translated by Hugh McDonald. The Aquinas Translation Project. http://hosted.desales.edu/w4/philtheo/loughlin/ATP/index.html.
———. *Summa Theologica*. Translated by Fathers of the English Dominican Province. New York: Benziger, 1947.
Audi, Robert. *The Good in the Right: A Theory of Intuition and Intrinsic Value*. Princeton: Princeton University Press, 2004.
———. "Intuitions, Intuitionism, and Moral Judgment." In *The New Intuitionism*, edited by Jill Graper Hernandez, 171–98. London: Continuum International, 2011.
———. "Reason and Experience, Obligation and Value: An Introduction to the New Intuitionism." In *The New Intuitionism*, edited by Jill Graper Hernandez, 45–52. London: Continuum International, 2011.
Auestad, Lene. "Splitting, Attachment and Instrumental Rationality: A Re-View of Menzies Lyth's Social Criticism." *Psychoanalysis, Culture & Society* 16.4 (2011) 394–410.
Augustine. *The City of God*. Translated by Marcus Dods. Peabody, MA: Hendrickson, 2009.
———. *The Trinity*. Translated by Stephen McKenna. Boston: St. Paul's, 1965.
Baggett, David, and Jerry Walls. *Good God: The Theistic Foundations of Morality*. New York: Oxford University Press, 2011.
Barrett, C. K. *A Commentary on the Epistle to the Romans*. London: A. & C. Black, 1991.

Barth, Karl. *Church Dogmatics: The Doctrine of the Word of God; Prolegomena to Church Dogmatics. Part 1.* Translated by G. T. Thomson. Vol. 1. New York: T. & T. Clark, 1936.

Bassler, Jouette M. *Divine Impartiality: Paul and a Theological Axiom.* Chico, CA: Scholars, 1982.

Bauer, Walter, et al., eds. "Κατακρίνω." In *A Greek-English Lexicon of the New Testament and Other Early Christian Literature*, 519. Chicago: University of Chicago Press, 2000.

Bavinck, Herman. *Reformed Dogmatics: God and Creation.* Edited by John Bolt, translated by John Vriend. Vol. 2 of 4 vols. Grand Rapids: Baker Academic, 2004.

———. *Reformed Dogmatics: Sin and Salvation in Christ.* Edited by John Bolt, translated by John Vriend. Vol. 3 of 4 vols. Grand Rapids: Baker Academic, 2006.

Berger, Peter L. *The Sacred Canopy: Elements of a Sociological Theory of Religion.* New York: Doubleday, 1967.

Bloom, Allan. *The Closing of the American Mind.* New York: Simon and Schuster, 1987.

Boa, Kenneth. *Faith Has Its Reasons: Integrative Approaches to Defending the Christian Faith.* Downers Grove: InterVarsity, 2001.

Bonaventure. *Opera Theologica Selecta.* Vol. 2. Quarrachi: Collegium S. Bonaventurae, 1934.

Bouwman, G. "Noch Einmal Römer 1,21–32." *Biblica* 54 (1973) 411–14.

Bruce, F. F. *The Letter of Paul to the Romans: An Introduction and Commentary.* Leicester, UK: InterVarsity, 1985.

Byrne, Brendan. *Romans.* Collegeville, MN: Liturgical, 1996.

Calvin, John. *Commentary on the Epistle of Paul the Apostle to the Romans.* Translated by John Owen. Vol. 19. Grand Rapids: Baker, 2003.

———. *The Epistles of Paul the Apostle to the Romans and to the Thessalonians.* Translated by Ross Mackenzie. Calvin's Commentaries. Grand Rapids: Eerdmans, 1960.

———. *Institutes of the Christian Religion.* Edited by John McNeill. Translated by Ford Lewis Battles. Philadelphia: Westminster, 1960.

Campbell, Constantine R. *Basics of Verbal Aspect in Biblical Greek.* Grand Rapids: Zondervan, 2008.

Chapman, John C. *Know and Tell the Gospel: The Why and How of Evangelism.* Sydney: Hodder & Stoughton, 1981.

Comfort, Ray. *God Doesn't Believe in Atheists: Proof That the Atheist Doesn't Exist.* Gainesville: Bridge-Logos, 1993.

Cowan, Steven B. "Five Views on Apologetics—Introduction." In *Five Views on Apologetics*, edited by Steven B. Cowan, 7–20. Grand Rapids: Zondervan, 2000.

Craig, William Lane. "Classical Apologetics." In *Five Views on Apologetics*, edited by Steven B. Cowan, 26–55. Grand Rapids: Zondervan, 2000.

———. "The Kurtz/Craig Debate: Is Goodness without God Good Enough?" In *Is Goodness without God Good Enough? A Debate on Faith, Secularism, and Ethics*, edited by Robert K. Garcia and Nathan L. King, 25–48. Plymouth: Rowman & Littlefield, 2009.

———. *Reasonable Faith: Christian Truth and Apologetics.* 3rd ed. Wheaton: Crossway, 2008.

Cranfield, C. E. B. *A Critical and Exegetical Commentary on the Epistle to the Romans: Introduction and Commentary on Romans I–VIII, Vol. 1*. 6th ed. Edinburgh: T. & T. Clark, 1975.

Daxer, Heinrich. *Römer 1.18–2.10 im Verhältnis zu Spätjüdischen Lehrauffassung*. Naumburg: Patz'sche, 1914.

Denney, James. "St. Paul's Epistle to the Romans." In *The Expositor's Greek Testament Volume Two*, edited by W. Robertson Nicoll, 555–725. Grand Rapids: Eerdmans, 1979.

Donaldson, Terence. *Paul and the Gentiles: Remapping the Apostle's Convictional World*. Minneapolis: Fortress, 1997.

Dulles, Avery. *A History of Apologetics*. 3rd ed. San Francisco: Ignatius, 2005.

Dunn, James D. G. *Romans 1–8*. Dallas: Word, 1988.

Edwards, Jonathan. "Miscellanies." In *The Philosophy of Jonathan Edwards*, edited by Harvey G. Townsend. Westport: Greenwood, 1972.

———. *The Power of God: A Jonathan Edwards Commentary on the Book of Romans*. Edited by David S. Lovi and Benjamin Westerhoff. Cambridge: Lutterworth, 2013.

Farrer, Austin. "In His Image." In *Remembering C. S. Lewis: Recollections of Those Who Knew Him*, edited by James T. Como, 344–45. 3rd ed. San Francisco: Ignatius, 2005.

Fischer, John Martin. "Frankfurt-Type Examples and Semi-Compatibilism." In *The Oxford Handbook of Free Will*, edited by Robert Kane, 281–308. New York: Oxford University Press, 2002.

Fitzmyer, Joseph A. *Romans: A New Translation with Introduction and Commentary*. New York: Doubleday, 1993.

Flanagan, Laura Melano. "Object Relations Theory." In *Inside Out and Outside In: Psychodynamic Clinical Theory and Psychopathololgy in Contemporary Multicultural Contexts*, 3rd ed., 118–57. Plymouth: Rowman & Littlefield, 2011.

Frame, John. *Apologetics to the Glory of God: An Introduction*. Phillipsburg, NJ: P & R, 1994.

———. *The Doctrine of the Knowledge of God*. Phillipsburg, NJ: Presbyterian & Reformed, 1987.

———. "Levels of Ethical Evaluation." *Reformed Perspectives Magazine* 1.19 (1999) n.p.

Freud, Sigmund. *Moses and Monotheism*. New York: Vintage, 1939.

Gerrish, B. A. "Errors and Insights in the Understanding of Revelation: A Provisional Response." *The Journal of Religion* 78.1 (1998) 64–88.

Godet, F. *Commentary on St. Paul's Epistle to the Romans*. Edited by T. W. Chambers. Grand Rapids: Kregel, 1977.

Groothius, Douglas. *Christian Apologetics: A Comprehensive Case for Biblical Faith*. Downers Grove: InterVarsity, 2011.

Haidt, Jonathan. *The Righteous Mind: Why Good People Are Divided By Politics and Religion*. New York: Vintage, 2012.

Halsey, J. S. *For a Time Such as This*. Nutley, NJ: Presbyterian & Reformed, 1978.

Hanna, Mark. *Crucial Questions in Apologetics*. Michigan: Baker, 1981.

Helm, Paul. "Calvin and Natural Law." *The Scottish Bulletin of Evangelical Theology* 2 (1984) 5–22.

Hendriksen, William. *Romans: Chapters 1–8*. Vol. 1. Edinburgh: Banner of Truth Trust, 1982.

Hill, Graham. *Salt, Light, and a City: Introducing Missional Ecclesiology*. Eugene, OR: Wipf and Stock, 2012.
Hooker, Morna. "Adam in Romans i." *New Testament Studies* 6.4 (1960) 297–306.
Hopkins, Samuel. *The Works of Samuel Hopkins*. Vol. 1 of 3 vols. Boston: Doctrinal Tract and Book Society, 1854.
Huemer, Michael. *Ethical Intuitionism*. Hampshire: Palgrave MacMillan, 2005.
Jewett, Robert. *Romans*. Augsburg: Fortress, 2007.
Johnson, S. Lewis, Jr. "Paul and the Knowledge of God." *Bibliotheca Sacra* 129.513 (1972) 61–74.
Käsemann, Ernst. *Commentary on Romans*. Grand Rapids: Eerdmans, 1982.
Keck, Leander E. *Romans*. Nashville: Abingdon, 2005.
Keener, Craig S. *Romans*. Eugene, OR: Cascade, 2009.
Kilcullen, Rupert John. "Natural Law." In *Encyclopedia of Medieval Philosophy*, edited by Henrik Lagerlund, 1:831–39. Dordrecht: Springer, 2011.
Klein, Melanie. "Love, Guilt and Reparation." In *Love, Guilt and Reparation and Other Works 1921–1945*, 306–43. London: Delacorte, 1937.
———. "Notes on Some Schizoid Mechanisms." *The International Journal of Psycho-Analysis* 27 (1946) 99–110.
———. "Some Theoretical Conclusions Regarding the Emotional Life of the Infant." In *The Collected Works of Melanie Klein*, 3:61–94. London: Hogarth, 1975.
Klostermann, E. "Die Adäquate Vergeltung in Rm 1,22–31." *Zeitschrift Für Die Neutestamentliche Wissenschaft* 32 (1933) 1–6.
Kruse, Colin. *Paul's Letter to the Romans*. Grand Rapids: Eerdmans, 2012.
Leithart, Peter. *Delivered from the Elements of the World: Atonement, Justification, Mission*. Downers Grove, 2016.
Levison, John. "Adam and Eve in Romans 1.18–25 and the Greek Life of Adam and Eve." *New Testament Studies* 50.4 (2004) 519–34.
Lewis, C. S. *Surprised by Joy: The Shape of My Early Life*. Orlando: Harcourt, 1955.
Liddell, H. G., and R. Scott. *A Greek-English Lexicon; with a Supplement*. Oxford: Clarendon, 1983.
———. "Ἀναπολογέομαι." In *A Greek-English Lexicon; with a Supplement*, 207–8. Oxford: Clarendon, 1968.
Lindbeck, George A. *The Nature of Doctrine: Religion and Theology in a Postliberal Age*. Philadelphia: Westminster, 1984.
Luther, Martin. *Commentary on Romans*. Translated by J. Theodore Mueller. Grand Rapids: Kregel, 1976.
———. *Lectures on Romans*. Edited and translated by Wilhelm Pauck. Louisville: Westminster John Knox, 2006.
———. *Luther's Works*. St. Louis: Concordia, 1955.
Matera, Frank J. *Romans*. Grand Rapids: Baker Academic, 2010.
McGrath, Alister E. *Mere Apologetics: How to Help Seekers and Skeptics Find Faith*. Grand Rapids: Baker, 2012.
———. *Surprised by Meaning: Science, Faith and How We Make Sense of Things*. Louisville: Westminster John Knox, 2011.
Meissner, W. W. *Psychoanalysis and Religious Experience*. Ann Arbor: Edwards Brothers, 1984.
Meyer, Heinrich. *Critical and Exegetical Handbook to the Epistle to the Romans*. Translated by J. C. Moore. Edinburgh: T. & T. Clark, 1876.

Michel, Otto. *Der Brief an die Römer*. Göttingen: Vandenhoeck & Ruprecht, 1978.
Middendorf, Michael P. *Romans 1–8*. St. Louis: Concordia, 2013.
Moo, Douglas J. *The Epistle to the Romans*. Grand Rapids: Eerdmans, 1996.
Moreland, James Porter, and William Lane Craig. *Philosophical Foundations for a Christian Worldview*. Downers Grove: IVP Academic, 2003.
Morley, B. K. *Mapping Apologetics: Comparing Contemporary Approaches*. Downers Grove: InterVarsity, 2015.
Morris, L. L. *The Epistle to the Romans*. Grand Rapids: Eerdmans, 1988.
Murray, John. *The Epistle to the Romans: The English Test with Introduction, Exposition and Notes*. Vol. 1–2. Grand Rapids: Eerdmans, 1968.
Newbigin, Lesslie. *The Gospel in a Pluralist Society*. Grand Rapids: Eerdmans, 1989.
———. *Truth to Tell: The Gospel as Public Truth*. Grand Rapids: Eerdmans, 1991.
Ockham, William. *Commentary on the Sentences of Peter Lombard*, 1318. Public domain e-book. N.p.
O'Donovan, Oliver. *Resurrection and Moral Order: An Outline for Evangelical Ethics*. Leicester, UK: InterVarsity, 1986.
Osborne, Grant R. *Romans*. Downers Grove: InterVarsity, 2004.
Owen, H. P. "The Scope of Natural Revelation in Rom. i and Acts Xvii." *New Testament Studies* 5 (1958) 133–43.
Pannenberg, Wolfhart. *Systematic Theology*. Translated by Geoffrey Bromiley. Vol. 1. Grand Rapids: Eerdmans, 1991.
Pauck, Wilhelm, ed. *Melanchthon and Bucer*. Library of Christian Classics 19. Philadelphia: Westminster, 1969.
Peirce, Charles S. *Collected Papers*. Edited by Charles Hartshorne and Paul Weiss. Vol. 5. Cambridge, MD: Harvard University Press, 1960.
Polanyi, Michael. *Knowing and Being*. Edited by Marjorie Grene. London: Routledge and Kegan Paul, 1969.
———. *Personal Knowledge: Towards a Post-Critical Philosophy*. Chicago: University of Chicago Press, 1962.
Popkes, W. "Zum Aufbau und Charakter von Römer 1.18 32." *New Testament Studies* 28 (1982) 490–501.
Putnam, Hilary. "The Meaning of 'Meaning.'" In *Philosophical Papers, Vol. 2: Mind, Language and Reality*, 215–71. Cambridge: Cambridge University Press, 1975.
Räisänen, Heikki. *Paul and the Law*. Philadelphia: Fortress, 1986.
———. *The Torah and Christ: Essays in German and English on the Problem of the Law in Early Christianity*. Helsinki: Finnish Exegetical Society, 1986.
Reymond, Robert. *A New Systematic Theology of the Christian Faith*. Nashville: Thomas Nelson, 1998.
Rizzuto, Ana-Maria. *The Birth of the Living God*. London: University of Chicago Press, 1979.
Ross, W. D. *The Right and the Good*. Oxford: Oxford University Press, 1930.
Salmon, Wesley C. "Religion and Science: A New Look at Hume's Dialogues." *Philosophical Studies* 33.2 (1978) 143–76.
Sanday, William, and Arthur Cayley Headlam. *A Critical and Exegetical Commentary on the Epistle to the Romans*. Edinburgh: T. & T. Clark, 1902.
Sanders, E. P. *Paul, the Law, and the Jewish People*. Minneapolis: Fortress, 1983.

Schaff, Philip, ed. "The Belgic Confession. A.D. 1561. Revised 1619." In *The Creeds of Christendom with a History and Critical Notes*, 4th ed, 383–436. Grand Rapids: Baker, 1977.

Schreiner, Thomas R. "Did Paul Believe in Justification by Works? Another Look at Romans 2." *Bulletin of Biblical Research* 3 (1993) 131–55.

———. *Romans*. Grand Rapids: Baker, 1998.

Schrenk, Gottlob. "Δικαίωμα." In *Theological Dictionary of the New Testament*, 2:174–224. Grand Rapids: Eerdmans, 1964.

Schulz, S. "Die Anklage in Röm 1,18–32." *Theologische Zeitschrift* 14 (1958) 161–73.

Scotus, Duns. *Duns Scotus on the Will and Morality*. Edited by William Frank, translated by Allan Wolter. Washington: Catholic University of America Press, 1986.

Sinnott-Armstrong, Walter. "Reflections on Reflection in Robert Audi's Moral Intuitionism." In *Rationality and the Good: Critical Essays on the Ethics and Epistemology of Robert Audi*, edited by Mark Timmons et al., 19–30. Oxford: Oxford University Press, 2007.

Spero, Moshe Halevi. *Religious Objects as Psychological Structures: A Critical Integration of Object Relations Theory, Psychotherapy, and Judaism*. Chicago: University of Chicago Press, 1992.

Sproul, R. C., et al. *Classical Apologetics*. Grand Rapids: Zondervan, 1984.

Stowers, Stanley Kent. *The Diatribe and Paul's Letter to the Romans*. Chico, CA: Scholars, 1981.

Stratton-Lake, Philip, ed. *Ethical Intuitionism: Re-Evaluations*. Oxford: Oxford University Press, 2002.

St. Vincent Millay, Edna. "Upon This Age That Never Speaks Its Mind." In *Collected Sonnets*, 140. New York: Harper Perennial, 1988.

Taylor, James E. *Introducing Apologetics: Cultivating Christian Commitment*. Grand Rapids: Baker Academic, 2006.

Thiselton, Anthony C. *Discovering Romans: Content, Interpretation, Reception*. Grand Rapids: Eerdmans, 2016.

Urmson, J. "Saints and Heroes." In *Essays in Moral Philosophy*, edited by A Melden, 198–216. Seattle: University of Washington Press, 1958.

VanDrunen, David. *Natural Law and the Two Kingdoms: A Study in the Development of Reformed Social Thought*. Grand Rapids: Eerdmans, 2010.

Vanhoozer, Kevin J. "Theology and the Condition of Postmodernity." In *The Cambridge Companion to Postmodern Theology*, edited by Kevin J. Vanhoozer, 3–25. Cambridge: Cambridge University Press, 2003.

Van Til, Cornelius. *An Introduction to Systematic Theology*. Phillipsburg, NJ: Presbyterian & Reformed, 1974.

Wallace, Daniel B. *Greek Grammar Beyond the Basics*. Grand Rapids: Zondervan, 1996.

Windsor, Lionel. "Paul and the Vocation of Israel: How Paul's Jewish Identity Informs His Apostolic Ministry, with Special Reference to Romans." PhD Thesis, Durham University, 2012. http://etheses.dur.ac.uk/3920/.

Witherington, Ben, III, and Darlene Hyatt. *Paul's Letter to the Romans: A Socio-Rhetorical Commentary*. Grand Rapids: Eerdmans, 2004.

Zahn, Theodor. *Der Brief des Paulus an die Römer*. Leipzig: Deichert, 1910.

Zeller, Dieter. *Der Brief an die Römer*. Regensburg: Pustet, 1985.

www.ingramcontent.com/pod-product-compliance
Lightning Source LLC
Chambersburg PA
CBHW050835160426
43192CB00010B/2032